THE ART OF OCCULTISM

The Secrets of High Occultism & Inner Exploration

Gabriyell Sarom

Copyright © 2018 - Gabriyell Sarom

First Edition
ISBN: 9781792786082

Design: Barandash Karandashich & Katja Gerasimova/shutterstock

All rights reserved, including those of translation into other languages. Except for use in a review, no part of this book may be reproduced in any form or by any means, electronic or mechanical, including scanning, uploading, photocopying, recording, or by any information storage and retrieval system, without permission in writing from the author or the publisher. The information herein is not intended to replace the services of trained health professionals or be a substitute for medical advice. The reader is advised to consult with his health care professional with regard to matters relating to his health, and in particular regarding matters that may require diagnosis or medical attention. The meditations shared here should not be followed without first consulting a health care professional. This book is published and sold with the understanding that the author and publisher are not engaged in rendering legal, medical, or other professional services by reason of their authorship or publication of this work. If medical or other expert assistance is required, the services of a competent professional person should be sought.

Contents

	Introduction	9
SECTION 1	**ENLIGHTENING THE OCCULT**	**11**
Chapter 1	What is Occultism?	13
Chapter 2	Why Does the World Reject Occultism?	17
Chapter 3	Beyond the Seen	21
Chapter 4	The Symbolism of the Human Being	25
Chapter 5	The Subconscious Mind	27
SECTION 2	**THE SEVEN FOUNDATIONS OF HIGH OCCULTISM**	**31**
Chapter 6	I – The Primordial Substance	33
Chapter 7	II – What God Is	37
Chapter 8	III – First-Hand Experience	41
Chapter 9	IV – Creation is a Thought	45
Chapter 10	V – Cause and Effect	49
Chapter 11	VI – The Same Spectrum	51
Chapter 12	VII – Mind-Control	55
SECTION 3	**OCCULT PRACTICE**	**59**
Chapter 13	The Practices of High Occultism	61

	Preparation	64
	Phase One: Laboratorium	68
	Phase Two: Steady Inner & Outer Gaze	72
	Phase Three: Burning the Shadow of Fear	84
	Phase Four: Infusing Vital Energy	93
	Phase Five: Inner Laboratorium	101
	Divine Infusion	112
	Inner Requests	113
	Phase Six: Inner Union	115
	Union with the Inner Master	115
	Beyond the Form of Divinity	117
Chapter 14	Interaction with Nonphysical Beings	119
	Evocations	125
SECTION 4	**GOING FORWARD**	**129**
Chapter 15	It is Not a Coincidence	131
Chapter 16	The High Occultist	135
	Epilogue	139
	Publications	141
	Suggested Reading	142

Publications

The Art of Mysticism

The Step-by-step practical guide to Mysticism & Spiritual Meditations

The Art of Magick

The Mystery of Deep Magick & Divine Rituals

Subscribe to Gabriyell Sarom's Newsletter and receive the book:

Divine Abilities: 3 Techniques to Awaken Divine Abilities

www.sacredmystery.org

Third-person singular pronoun use

Since there are recurrent references to "student", "practitioner" or to the "reader", which are interchangeable, and they require the use of third-person singular pronouns, and to avoid the repeated use of "he or she", "his or her" and "him or her", the author has utilized the traditional "he", "his" and "him" when referring to the "student", the "practitioner" and the "reader". In this case, "he" is not to be seen as male, and the author hopes that female students, practitioners and readers will comprehend this and not be offended.

Introduction

A colossal fence has been raised separating our current society from the flow of life and magic that permeates the whole of Creation. Humanity is gradually succeeding in its self-destruction, asphyxiating itself through the suppression of what is beyond the mere five physical senses. The art of Occultism has been forgotten.

In fact, Occultism has been despised, ridiculed and denigrated into mere fantasy, make-believe, or magical thinking. This book brings this ancient secret tradition back to life using a contemporary yet powerful method.

As the illustrious offspring of modern materialistic science and reason, we have entirely forgotten our ancestral divine knowledge. The apparent disintegration of the unified field of All That Is is the standard of virtue that we, as humans, seem to live by. Despite this affront, that which is occult is unperturbed by humanity and its physical, energetic, and mental pollution.

To fulfill our destiny, the riddle of life and death must be solved, and this can only be accomplished by seeing beyond what we are conditioned to see. We must find the hidden dimension of life which is to be brought to light within ourselves.

This is a book centered on occult practices. It intends to make the occult visible yet again. We will lay down the mystery of the hidden dimension of life, encouraging you and showing you the means by which you can discover it. Here the reader will find detailed occult practices that will assist him in exploring the subtle inner nonphysical realms, culminating in the unveiling of the highest mystery of Occultism.

Mankind must finally abandon the ignorant perspective it has held for thousands of years, and uncover an unhampered display of extraordinary divinity. We sincerely hope the reader enjoys this work and that it may serve as the catalyst for this discovery.

SECTION 1

Enlightening the Occult

1

What is Occultism?

Usually, Occultism is associated with something obscure. In fact, it's easy to find something dark associated with Occultism in books or on the internet.

If someone ever brings up this subject, people will feel uncomfortable and frown in disapproval. It is quite a controversial theme.

Notwithstanding, the quintessence of Occultism could not be further from "darkness". That is not what it means.

Focused upon the physical realm, human beings have limited their self-knowledge to their bodies, their perceived sensations, and their thoughts. Around themselves, they see a universe composed of physical matter with physical objects with which they (as a physical body) can interact. Is this all that exists? No, it is solely the tip of the iceberg.

Occultism goes well beyond the five physical senses, and more than being occult, it is ignored and overlooked.

Occultism is not the widely assumed practice that uses "spells", "potions", "dark" or "satanic" books, or just a figment of some lunatic's imagination which is permeated by ignorance. Because of charlatans and dogma-based secret societies, Occultism has been disproportionately demented as witchcraft, voodoo, demonic rituals, and so on. This is unequivocally not what Occultism is.

This book will not pursue frivolous endeavors that are usually coined "Occultism" but are no more than "New Age" creed, "sorcery" or poorly elaborated ceremonies that inaccurately pose as powerful attainments for the aspirant of Occultism.

What we deal with here is *High Occultism*, the authentic and original Occultism.

High Occultism is not related to spells, enchantments, sorcery, nor philters. It does not have the purpose of harming someone, attempting to gain a financial advantage in some business, infusing thoughts into others, or obtaining mystical superpowers solely for selfish exhibition. Such atrocious and ignoble practices only make the discovery of the Occult further and further away, strengthening egotism and ignorance. The legitimate Occultist is not a trickster nor an illusionist nor a circus performer.

High Occultism has the purpose of unveiling *The Occult* through the systematic practice of specific spiritual and mystical techniques, together with the inner exploration of subtle realms of consciousness.

But what is "The Occult"? It goes by many names: *The Primordial Substance; The Unified Field that Sustains Everything; All That Is; Spirit; God*, etc.

The true purpose of High Occultism is the unveiling of this ultimate mystery of Creation and the embodiment of "The Occult". There is indeed no more noble search than this one!

2

Why Does the World Reject Occultism?

Today's world rejects spirituality, Mysticism, Occultism, and anything in general that is beyond the typical materialistic paradigm. Our worldview, influenced by society and by the environment, circumstances and surroundings of our lives, dictates if we live by the prism of sadness or happiness.

This worldview is also shaped by our teachers, parents, and friends, by the press and commercial rhetoric which is constantly bombarding our ears and eyes, and by the culture in which each student is inserted. This makes the cultivation of an unprejudiced view of reality borderline impossible.

Such a stained view presupposes that what is real is what we can see, hear, touch, smell, or taste, while everything else is considered fantasy, a hallucination, a dream, an imagination, or a fairy-tale.

No student of Occultism doubts that society is regularly trying to impel its perspective concerning what is real, what we should do, think, and feel.

If humans live by the motto that "reality" consists solely of a physical universe with physical objects within it, they are no different than a frog that believes that the pond where it lives is all there is.

As if that were not enough, humans are constantly being inundated by advertisements (not just on TV but by close relatives and friends as well) demanding that we need those physical objects to be joyful and complete. Knowingly or unknowingly, we are pressured to go through formal education and pursue a job that allows us to purchase those very same objects in order to feel realized and fulfilled. At least that's what society seems to tell us.

In fact, humans love to pursue material success, and that's our gauge for a successful life. The whole of society is built upon this principle, and working long hours, sacrificing health and peace of mind to achieve those materialistic milestones is seen as an essential remedy to this feeling of insufficiency and dissatisfaction that all humans feel.

It is not understood that this feeling is because we are limiting our multi-dimensional being to its physical aspect while neglecting all its other broader facets. Through the exploration of our countless dimensions, we will eventually come to know something beyond the five senses: the "beyond" which seems to be occult for now. Acquiring and projecting value onto things that would otherwise be seen as entirely trivial is a useless pursuit because such things will never fill our ever-empty glass.

As a matter of fact, there is nothing wrong with buying objects or acquiring new "things". The dilemma is that no "thing" can truly satisfy a human's thirst.

The predominant view that matter is the primordial substance and that everything, even consciousness, the mind, and its mental factors, is the outcome of matter brings serious negative consequences to the student of Occultism. It can look harmless, but it is like a parasite.

The materialistic worldview is fundamentally against Occultism. This belief results in a narrow and limiting view on how a student relates to the world and to reality.

There are moments in life in which the universe provides someone with an experience that transcends the mere physical senses. It is in these moments that most people turn into religion, Mysticism, Occultism or spirituality; or they just brush it aside and keep living their mundane lives.

Nonetheless, these experiences of the "beyond" can indeed be brought about by meditation and by mystic and occult practice. That's the whole purpose!

Rather than staying confined to the limited materialistic view of the modern world, the student shall expand his limited horizon into divine territory. This volume will help to break the student's mental barriers and serve as a flashlight pointing directly into the student's core.

3

Beyond the Seen

Occultism is not a work of a lower nature. It rightly belongs on an equivalent level as other traditions that are considered "high-caliber", such as Buddhism or Patanjali's Yoga.

Anyone who is seeking more knowledge and understanding about himself, the universe, God, the nature of reality, etc., must at some point discern that our ordinary human perceptions don't translate the whole picture. The five physical senses are very limited, and this knowledge is not some modern theory or a radical new idea.

Take a look at the electromagnetic spectrum.

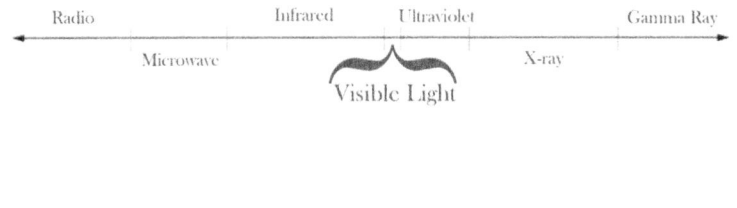
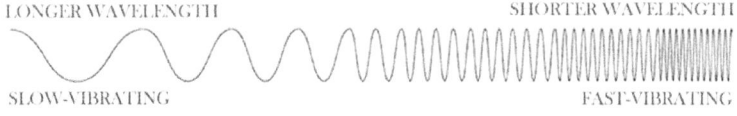

When we look at it, we can undeniably see that our limited physical senses are unable to directly perceive the tiny Visible Light range of the spectrum (from the color red to violet, including black, which absorbs all colors and reflects none, and white, which reflects all the colors), but our eyes cannot see X-ray, Gamma-ray, or Radio waves for example.

Different life forms have different capabilities. For example, bees and certain fish can perceive Ultraviolet light (humans also have the ability to see Ultraviolet light, but only if the eye's lens is removed); other animals, such as mice and cats, have their auditory capacity in a frequency different than those of humans, and are able to hear sounds that humans cannot.

This is discussed so that the student can understand that what he sees or perceives is not all there is. There is also the capacity to think and feel, which can be said to be extra senses. Ultimately, there are a multitude of things that escape our ability to perceive with our physical senses.

Whenever an aspirant experiences a nonphysical vision, hears a nonphysical sound, etc., he's not using his physical eyes or ears; he's actually using his mind's inherent and usually untapped power to access a broader spectrum of consciousness beyond physicality.

Some rare persons are born with these kinds of capacities, but for most of us, they are only obtained through rigorous dedication to occult and mystical practice.

Therefore, we have varying degrees of unveiling what is occult, that is, what is beyond the gross physical senses.

We go from being able to consciously use the five subtle senses to perceive the subtle dimensions of life, to ever more profound levels until we arrive at Infinity itself, God, the Highest Occult.

By embracing the practices presented in this volume, or by following the teachings of the book *The Art of Mysticism*, the student can unlock all the nuances and subtle levels of Occultism. The student must climb the various steps leading to the ultimate. The pace at which that is done depends on the diligence and determination of the student, and also on the relinquishing of the student's mundane and shallow way of living, acting, talking, and thinking.

High Occultism is a means to a new and greater existence, which unfolds once we delve into what is beyond the obvious. It is up to the student to decide to take the first step in this wondrous journey.

4

The Symbolism of the Human Being

The human being is the most divine symbol in Occultism. How so? The ancient traditions revealed the secret that the universal elements, hidden powers, and all mysteries of Creation are present in the human body and mind. Everything that exists outside Man has its equivalent within. This is the highest of symbolisms.

Our minds can create an entirely new universe in our imagination and dreams. We have that power, the power to create. The human body and mind are like sparks, while the universe is fire; or if you prefer a different analogy, we are tiny drops of water in the vast universal ocean of Creation.

This means that something as small as an atom has in itself the source code of the whole universe.

The universe, in its macrocosmic nature, inexhaustible in its vastness and mind-boggling in its mysteries, is incomprehensible to the human mind, so long as it confines itself to the physical senses. However, the microcosm, which is the universe inside us that mirrors the external universe, can be understood and realized through practice, contemplation, and meditation. The further our consciousness is from the physical senses, and the more engrossed it is in the subtle senses, the freer we are to assimilate the mysteries of Creation.

This is why students of Occultism use the mind as an instrument to explore and scrutinize the infinite inner world. In our own body and mind, we can find and unveil all universal mysteries. It is for this reason that mystical or occult practice is of so much importance. Investigating the external cosmos through the confined physical senses will lead to limited discoveries.

Fundamentally, no external endeavor can bring the ultimate knowledge of Man and Creation, nor can it bring lasting peace or allow Man to shape his own destiny. These achievements can only be found inside, by dissolving the mist that seems to cover that which is occult: God within.

Then, when the occult is unveiled, the genuine student will at last experience the cosmic ecstasy of union with God and realize that what once was thought to be occult, actually shines in full brilliance.

5

The Subconscious Mind

One of the most important discoveries a student of Occultism can make is to learn how to hone the potential of the subconscious mind. Connecting with the subconscious and learning how to unleash its power is a crucial milestone on the path of Occultism.

The student must not mistake the term "subconscious" from the perspective of Occultism with other definitions, such as those employed by some famous psychiatrists. There may be some similarities to the untrained eye, but the purpose and approach towards the subconscious by the student of Occultism is wholly different.

The mind may be only one, but to facilitate the student's

understanding, we must divide it into the conscious and the subconscious mind.

These two aspects manifest different characteristics. A whole book could be written about them, but we shall not pursue such endeavors because we only need an elementary conceptual understanding for the purposes of occult study and practice. We value practice and fieldwork over theory and scholarly work.

While the conscious mind deals with everything that is within the realm of your conscious awareness (including subjective experiences such as thoughts, feelings, etc.), the subconscious mind deals with everything that is within your psyche, yet below your conscious level. They are both parts of your consciousness, yet one is *directly* experienced day to day, while the other is *indirectly* experienced every day in addition to being directly experienced in dreams and in meditative and trance states.

The conscious mind deals with the five physical senses, while the subconscious mind with the nonphysical senses (e.g., intuition, clairvoyance, clairaudience, visions, mind reading, etc.).

The knowledge of the conscious mind is gathered through the five physical senses, while the knowledge of the subconscious mind is independent of them. While the first knowledge occurs only when a person is in waking consciousness, the second occurs during waking, dreaming, or meditative consciousness. Its recognition is enhanced whenever the objective world is in dormancy, such as when we are meditating, in a state of trance, right after waking up, or right before falling asleep.

By learning how to tap into the subconscious mind and use its power, which is inherent to every human being, the student experiences more creativity, energy, well-being, contentment, and wisdom. Even psychic abilities may manifest in our lives.

The subconscious mind is so powerful that it is an essential instrument on the path of the occultist. The student who has achieved the ability to deliberately use the subconscious' immense capabilities for spiritual benefit, as well as in day-to-day life, is indeed far along the journey of High Occultism.

The infinite intelligence of God greatly manifests through intuition and creativity in the subconscious mind. In humans, it lies mostly in potential, and for most people, it remains untapped throughout their lives. The student must start to connect his conscious mind with his subconscious mind, enabling him to expand further and deeper into this richer layer of the mind.

In the realm of the subconscious, things don't work as logically as on the conscious mind. The subconscious works more with visual imagery and symbols, and as we delve further into it, we will enter into subtle realms of ethereal imagery, archetypes, and powerful symbology. Interacting with the psyche and purifying it through such connection enables the student to recondition his behaviors, attitudes, thinking patterns, emotions regarding traumatic experiences, and even the unconscious detritus of past lives. It is powerful.

Subconscious work will also allow the student to be more receptive to new ideas, thoughts, understandings, and so on, imparting extraordinary inspiration to perform art, produce creative works in all fields, and receive knowledge regarding the different appearances in and facets of Creation. This process can reveal new previously unthought of perspectives. Furthermore, the student will be more appreciative of beauty, because the five physical senses will be infused with new fresh energy from the subtle senses.

The student of Occultism will also use the subconscious as a portal into the collective consciousness of humanity and even into the universal mind of God.

As your ability to pierce deeply into your own mind strengthens, in the company of your inner Master, your life's purpose may also be revealed to you. It is true that there are many determinants at play here, but clearing away mind blockages in the subconscious psyche is one of the most significant ones.

Be warned that this will not be a rapid process, but anything that comes quickly also departs quickly. Perseverance is a crucial skill in all aspects of life if one wants to be successful. In High Occultism, this attribute is even more necessary. All of this shall be made explicit through the appliance of occult practice which we'll disclose further down in the book.

SECTION 2

The Seven Foundations of High Occultism

6

I – The Primordial Substance

Spirit, God, Source, or the Primordial Substance is the underlying foundation or substance of all appearances, including those of a physical, energetic, mental, or causal nature. It is the Supreme Power. Everything that we call matter, energy, or thought has that which is occult as its foundation. This foundation, Spirit, or God, is inconceivable, unthinkable, and unknowable. It is the essential nature of all that exists.

In the Universe, everything is at all times becoming something, regardless of whether it is perceptible or not. Nothing is static; only change is constant.

This makes the rhythm of Creation, namely the ever-flowing breath of God, the only perpetual principle in Creation considering it is ever-going from its conception to its apparent finale.

This constant principle of change cannot endure without a primordial substance that sustains it, just like a drawing needs a paper as its support. Drawings may be continuously changing, but the underlying substance, the paper, is immutable, just like space is immutable yet functions as the base that allows objects to be.

This Primordial Substance, which we now know is that which is called God, is not an entity or an individual, although people all over the world attribute characteristics, features, emotions, traits, or even a personality to Him, including students of Occultism and Mysticism. Students of Occultism may see God with a form in the beginning, but as they progress on the path, God will resemble human form less and less, becoming ever more transparent, shapeless, and unknowable.

The dilemma with ascribing human qualities to the Primordial Substance is that, by doing so, we are impinging definitions and limits into what is essentially immeasurable and undefining.

It may seem harmless, but sooner or later, the human mind will deform this teaching, thereby attributing human qualities to God such as pride, envy, vengefulness, or being fond of adoration and so on. This is precisely what occurred with religions.

Students of Occultism should not pursue or feed such notions. It is for this reason that High Occultism teaches to see God as an abstract Golden Sphere of Light in the beginning. This enables the student's mind to internally interact with a non-embodied form of God, which is without traits, as opposed to having the form of a man, woman, angel, deva, animal, deity, or of any other being. More about this will be explained later on.

At the end of the day, communion with God is done through practice. We don't want to make the student seek knowledge within the boundaries of his intellect; we want the student to explore and inquire into the unknown, beyond the mere five senses and the mind, into the godly territory of the Occult.

II – What God Is

In the tradition of High Occultism, everything is considered to be God, the Primordial Substance. Therefore, there is nothing outside of God. God is both the All and the Nothing; He is infinite and eternal. Nothing can confine God because both "confined" and "liberated" are merely limited properties of a limited substance. That is, confining or liberating, ignorance or emancipation are just thoughts occurring within the dream of God. They cannot limit God but are part of His Creation.

God's power is infinite. Just like you have the power to create a universe out of nothing when you dream, regardless of the shape, contents, and so on, God has also infinite powers of creation.

God has never not been God. God cannot cease to be God, just like space cannot cease to be space, despite whatever objects you fill it up with. God is indeed pretty much like space: infinite, boundless, undestroyable, and the basis for everything.

God is not subject to anything. God is the rock, the one lifting it and the very act of successfully lifting it up. God is the rock, the one unable to lift it and the very act of failing to lift it up. God is truly limitless. He cannot be increased or decreased in any way, just like space. God will always and ever stay the same with no changes and no properties.

God's power is the Ultimate Force. Not some random force, but the supremely intelligent Force behind the creation, design, sustenance and eventually the end of the Universe as we know it. Matter is nothing but this Force in action; in movement. The faster the Force of God vibrates, the subtler the realm and its living beings and objects are; the slower the vibration, the grosser the realm and its living beings and objects are.

Here are the eight elementary facets of Existence and Creation in High Occultism:

0- Spirit (God-Consciousness) -> The Infinite, Immutable, All That Is, Eternity. God is not a byproduct of Creation.

1- Spirit's Breath (God-Force) -> The Constant, The Vibration that ever-changes, the Creative Power.

2- Mind -> Extremely subtle Vibration.

3- Space/Akasha/Ether -> Subtle Vibration.

4- Air/Gas -> Less Subtle Vibration.

5- Fire/Plasma -> Less subtle than Air (4), but still a fine Vibration.

6- Water/Liquid-> Less subtle than Fire (5), but finer than Earth's (7) grosser Vibration.

7- Earth/Solid -> Gross Vibration.

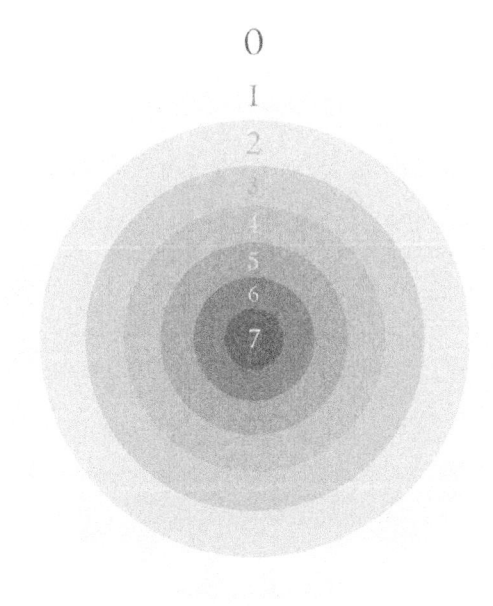

8

III – First-Hand Experience

The universal mind of God holds within itself all facets of our multidimensional Creation as if they were a dream, a thought, or an imagination. Only this universal mind can understand itself; that is, only God can understand Himself. It is unknowable to Man because Man utilizes his intellect as the grasping tool. Taking into consideration that God is actually All That Is, being the underlying principle, it encircles everything, including each one of us. For this reason, our innate unity with God is only blocked by our current state of ignorance.

This ignorance makes God, which is the only real and

timeless reality, appear to be non-existing. Therefore, God seems to be occult.

In High Occultism, we attempt to unravel this curtain of ignorance and become one with God, thus making the occult, non-occult.

Comprehending this teaching empowers the reader to realize the purpose of High Occultism. This is essential to progress on this path; the ultimate goal of High Occultism and the scope of the teachings in this volume are now clear beyond any doubt.

Although the understanding of this law is required, students should not create beliefs, assumptions, and conjectures regarding what God is because attempting to comprehend God through the limited human mind is merely a futile attempt at trying to understand Infinity through finite instruments. Logic, analysis, interpretations, thoughts, concepts, etc., are not suitable ways to discover God unless a student wants to run around in circles.

To know God is to experience first-hand what God is. If a student only reads and discusses about God, he will only read and discuss about God. If you want to embark on a journey on the Trans-Siberian Railway, you must go to Russia and board the train instead of reading brochures about it or seeing photographs and videos of the railway.

Only through mystical or occult practice can the student discover what God is by uniting with Him. Direct experience is the only remedy that cures the malady of ignorance.

Unveiling this secret, the student will crack open the

doors to the inner Self, the Temple of the Divine. Knowing that the whole of Creation is nothing more than the imagination of God, and is thus wholly mental, leads us to the next Foundation.

9

IV – Creation is a Thought

The idea that the universe is purely mental may not make much sense at first glance, but take into consideration the following: every time you fall asleep, you create an entirely new universe just as vivid as the physical universe where you consider yourself to be. This dream universe has its own atoms, solid matter, living beings, etc. But are they really physical, or are they solely mental, a creation of your mind? Upon waking, you know without any doubt that these lively dreams were all created by your mind.

Our universe works in the same way: it is only a creation of a mind. The difference is that our dream universe is a mental creation of our finite mind, while the universe we live in is a creation of the infinite mind of God.

In our world, people are usually taught to adhere to a collection of beliefs and assumptions that completely ignore the mystery of God, life, and existence. We live ensnared by the material world, binding and giving us no time to search for something more significant, to unveil the Occult.

While modern science is knowledgeable about everything pertaining to materialism, postulating that matter is the primordial substance and mind and consciousness its byproducts, the ancient mystics and masters of Occultism were the owners of transcendental wisdom that goes beyond both the blind materialistic paradigm and the five physical senses.

Given the mental nature of the universe, that which is considered "material" is a byproduct of what is actually a mental phenomenon. This implies that by having perfect control of all that is mental, one can have absolute control of all that is physical. This inherent power in human beings is not easily achievable and requires years of practice, dedication, and hard work.

The power to drastically shape this dimension is remarkably rare, despite there being various ancient tales of its use. It might be hard for the ordinary person—and even for students of Mysticism and Occultism—to distinguish between which tales are real and which are bogus. This capability to discriminate arises within a practitioner who has himself displayed such powers or witnessed someone using them.

Despite what the student may read in books of Occultism, bending this physical reality is not easy. This is because there are diverse factors at play:

- both the conscious and subconscious capacity of the student (just believing it will happen with the conscious mind isn't enough because the subconscious mind is much more powerful as a reservoir of subtle intentions and mental abilities);

- the degree of difficulty of what the student is trying to accomplish;

- the destiny of the student attempting to do it;

- the destiny of those affected by whatever the student is seeking to manifest;

- the lessons that the student has to learn (e.g., someone attempting to bend this reality for personal gain may meet failure and subsequently learn that the correct occult path is not one of egotism, but rather one of expansion and union with All That Is).

And even if the student succeeds, it will have taken much effort, time, and numerous attempts. The less "friction" there is to what is trying to be achieved, the easier it will be. Friction is caused by the degree of impediment or facilitation of the several factors mentioned above.

This is where notions such as the "Law of Attraction"

arise. The Law of Attraction is just an attempt to manifest or bend the reality towards what one wishes. It is an endeavor to solidify our thoughts in the physical realm.

If it's something easily achievable, with no impact on the destiny of the student of Occultism or of others, such as finding a one-dollar bill, it may take minutes, hours, or a few days to attract or manifest such an intent. But if it's something truly improbable, such as winning the lottery, it may never happen. This would be because of the factors mentioned above. No one can expect to be able to manifest whatever he wishes just by using the Law of Attraction.

Low-impact intentions are easier to manifest and require less mental power than High-impact intentions. The latter happens progressively and requires enormous mystical power. It can happen faster, but only a genuine Mystic or Occultist is capable of doing so.

Ultimately, the failure to recognize the mental nature of the universe is due to an overdependence on the five physical senses. Are they the measure of what's real? As we've already seen, they are not. Vast potential lies beyond the drylands of the physical senses, namely freedom from the cage of this physical body—indeed, this is the ultimate freedom.

10

V – Cause and Effect

This principle states that nothing in Creation is motionless. There's always movement—a force, an action, a response, a reaction, an ascending and descending, something that arises and then disappears, etc. Beings are born into life and sink into death.

In Creation, everything has a cause and an effect. Nothing occurs without a cause. The ultimate causeless cause is God. All things are an effect of God, and the chain reaction endures infinitely.

Coincidences are nonexistent because everything is a flower that has a preceding seed. The egg is the effect of the hen, and the hen the cause of the egg. But at the same time, the hen is an effect of the egg, and the egg the cause of the hen. But which came first?

If we go back, we see that it is God who is first. God, being the Primordial Substance, didn't come from anywhere. He always is, and time doesn't confine Him. Therefore, He cannot come or be born.

The first ever chicken came from an egg from another species that could be called the "parent species" of the chicken. If we go further back in the chain of evolution, we will eventually arrive at the first-ever form of life on this planet. Prior to that lifeform, there was no physical life on this planet, but the building blocks of life were present.

If we recede even more, billions of years, we will at last arrive at the Big Bang, the origin of the Universe. If we attempt to go beyond this point, there is no more going back, because the Big Bang was the beginning of time itself. But what was the ultimate cause of the Big Bang? God, the Primordial Substance, the Unknowable and Undefinable, because God is outside time.

To go above cause and effect, we have to go beyond the bounds of the causal plane (space-time). The discovery and union with the Primordial Substance is how the Occultist gains the way out of this infinite chain reaction of cause-effect.

This union requires the identification and understanding of the twofold nature of Creation, and the need to implode this polarity. That's the next step.

11

VI – The Same Spectrum

There is no black without white, left without right, high without low, above without below, distant without near, beginning without end, beauty without ugliness, sweet without bitter, silence without noise, positive without negative, here without there, joy without sorrow, success without failure, life without death, etc.

In Creation, there is always an opposite because everything has its counterpart. There is a positive pole and a negative pole; or in other words, there is a masculine pole and a feminine pole. They complete each other. These two energies, which are essentially one (God) have been separated so that Creation could come forth.

They are facets of the same spectrum, for they bear the same essential nature. Take the example of "short" and "tall". Can you pinpoint where tall starts? Or when does it stop being tall and begins to be short? Where is the line that separates both?

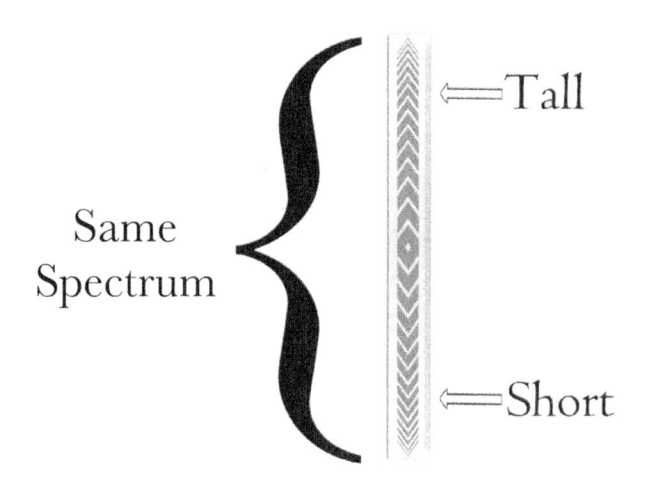

Same Spectrum { ⇐ Tall / ⇐ Short

They are differing grades of the same endless spectrum. This principle of height, which is just an illustration, is what may manifest with different degrees of vibration which we would call tall or short. Furthermore, what is tall and short is always contingent upon the subject in question. A 7ft/2.13m man is tall, but a giraffe with the same height would be considered exceptionally small; a 5ft/1.52m man is short, but a tortoise with the same height (giant tortoise) would be regarded as exceptionally big.

The road up and the road down are the same thing.

— Hippolytus, Refutations 9.10.3

While there are opposites, there will be duality, manifestation, creation, ups and downs, birth and death, etc. The real unveiling of the Occult is only attainable by merging these two poles—these two energies.

They go by distinct names in diverse traditions and cultures: Jachin and Boaz, Shiva and Shakti, Yin and Yang, Sun and the Moon, Father and Mother, Yab and Yum, Masculine and Feminine energy, the left and right hemispheres of the brain, positive and negative polarities, etc.

When masculine and feminine unite, the essence of the Occult is revealed: Oneness or Union with God. There, opposites merge and all paradoxes are settled.

For instance, let us delve into light and darkness. Upon close examination, the student will realize that there is no darkness, only different degrees of light. The more absent light is, the greater the darkness. This means that they are differing grades amid two extremities of the same phenomena. Just like darkness is simply the absence of light, hot and cold, for example, are solely different degrees of the spectrum of temperature. This applies to all aspects of Creation, from the physical dimension to the astral and mental.

Now here comes the occult law: if extremes are both part of the same spectrum, and if this applies to the physical dimension as well as to the astral and mental dimensions, then we can use the process of spiritual alchemy through occult practice to transition from being restless to peaceful; from being fearful to courageous; from being sad to joyful, from being ignorant to being enlightened.

Although these mental states appear to be entirely dissimilar, as the reader has realized by now, they are within the same spectrum! The reader can, therefore, alter the frequency from a negative state to a positive state.

The energy emanating from the mystic or occultist will also enable him to mentality affect and even change the vibrations of others. This is why many students feel a mighty vibration when near a legitimate Mystic or Occultist. The Master's pure vibrations affect the state of the disciples, pulling them into his own energetic field.

Notwithstanding, there is one secret within this occult principle that completely surpasses it: God. God has no opposite because God has no qualities or characteristics. God is thus beyond the dualism of life.

12

VII – Mind-Control

People all over the world seem to have become slaves to their minds. Their actions do not come from a position of clarity, but instead, they come from the whirlwind of emotions, desires, and confused thoughts.

It is often said that dogs are humans' best friends. Sometimes dogs are wild like wolves; other times they behave well but don't understand or obey our commands. However, a well-trained dog will do whatever his owner asks him. That dog is well-behaved and would do anything for his owner. The mind must be like that beloved dog.

For that to happen, the mind must be brought under control. The student has to become the master of his own mind. Before any action or speech are manifested, they first go through the mind. If the water in the lake of our mind is not still, it will poorly reflect the moonlight. If, on the other hand, the student learns how to still it, the reflection will be pure and perfect.

Countless methods attempt to make the mind tranquil and pure: occult and mystical practice, meditation, yoga, asceticism, fasting, etc. Some are more extreme than others and should not be attempted by unprepared students.

In this volume, we teach the way of the occultist, starting by purifying the mind, and only when it is brought under the student's control, will it be employed for our primary objectives.

The mind is governed by desire. If parents don't give a spoiled child the toy she demands, that child will be in tears to get it. As soon as she gets it, she will become satisfied. This satisfaction, however, only lasts a short amount of time, and soon the pampered child will ask for a new one, or even start crying again. The human mind is like this spoiled child that does what she wants without respecting or obeying her parents, always looking for things to fulfill its ever-small span of attention and short-lived gratification.

This behavior does not change in grown-ups, seeing that they too spend their hard-earned income on useless gratification toys that soon become old-fashioned, consequently requiring the purchase of new toys. The mind will always look for ways to consummate its ardent desires, and it will not become still. This reveals itself as a big problem whenever a student wants to practice Occultism or meditation. It is indeed one of the hardest barriers to break through, and one of the most critical.

Occultism requires a high degree of concentration and selective attention, and that's the first step on the path towards becoming an adept. When you first attempt to practice, the mind will not forgive you. Be sure to expect a myriad of thoughts, imagery, drowsiness, dullness, boredom, lethargy, monotony, yawning, sleepiness, etc.

Our everyday lifestyle doesn't help. The student will not find straightforward success if he persists in leading a stressful life, always entangled in uncontrollable thinking or attempting to solve arduous intellectual and complex problems during the day. No one should expect to arrive home after such a day and perform a triumphant occult practice. Unfortunately, it is not that easy.

The student should aim to maintain a quiet state of mind during the day. This will make the transition from a "normal" state of consciousness to a "meditative" state of consciousness less turbulent whenever it is time to practice. However, that is not attainable by those who are just starting.

Therefore, to help with this transition, we will show the student how to prepare and energetically charge a special location of his choice to be used solely for occult practice. That will make an exceptional difference, and it's what we'll explain in the next section of this book.

SECTION 3

Occult Practice

13

The Practices of High Occultism

Occult practice encapsulates the implementation of four core skills: the power of attention, the ability to imagine, the ability to feel and put emotion into the practice, and the power of intent. Students usually perform rituals because these ceremonies help to improve three factors:

1. Imagination, because these students let themselves unite with the act, believing that what they are doing is a symbolic representation of the outcome they are looking for;

2. Emotion (same reason as point 1).

3. Attention, because their mind withdraws from the usual thoughts and distractions and becomes immersed in the act.

Notwithstanding, an intense and meticulous practice of rituals is not exactly needed, and can even become a distraction. Many students fall in love with rituals and never go past the act. It must be understood that regardless of how intricate rituals may be and how flawlessly they have been executed, they are merely a build-up to the main occult practice.

We will, however, employ the use of a "mini-ritual", which consists of preparing the mind for a deeper dive into its own inner kingdom.

The core of Occultism is realized through occult practice. Through it, a student can learn how to:

a) Cultivate the power of attention and imagination;

b) Acquire tremendous skill in the control of the vital force, the mind, and emotions;

c) Develop his ability to direct his conscious and subconscious intentions.

These are crucial skills in High Occultism, and they will be used to help the student explore the subtle astral and mental realms within.

High Occultism shares some practices with mysticism, as they have been presented in the book *The Art of Mysticism*. If you favor a mystical approach, use *The Art of Mysticism;* if you favor the path of a High Occultist, use this book.

Both traditions have similarities. Mysticism uses the power of attention, the control of the breath and of the vital force, and employs sacred syllables and visualizations together with passive observing awareness to achieve its purpose of Union with God.

High Occultism utilizes the power of imagination in conjunction with concentration as portals to explore both our own subconscious mind and the subtle dimensions of collective consciousness. From there it goes deeper into revealing the manifold mysteries of The Occult, from form to the void of formlessness, until the Primordial Substance stands revealed.

The following practices will require authentic dedication, disciplined application of the techniques, and an effort to sculpt one's own lifestyle to be more in harmony with this pursuit and journey.

Some, who may naturally be more advanced, might experience results quicker, but most will have to resolutely work to achieve life-changing results. These will come, but only for committed students.

Preparation

As a preparation for the following phases, the student should do a small practice of training the control of his awareness. This will help to interiorize the mind so that it is less affected by external noise and physical sensations. It can be practiced anywhere (indoors and outdoors) at any time.

The majority of people have been habituated since an early age to be only aware of what is external, becoming unconsciously addicted to external stimulus.

Learning how to become unconcerned by and disengaged from the external world is very important in the initial stages of Occultism. After much practice, this will become an instinctive reflex, and you won't need to spend much more time and attention into to erasing outside disturbances because they will instantly disappear once you are proficient in focusing your attention.

Instead of forcing the mind to ignore the input of the physical senses during practice, you will do the opposite: you will actually put your attention on them until the mind loses its interest.

a)

1. Sit comfortably in a straight-backed chair, sofa, mat, or on a meditation cushion. Find an enjoyable position and stay there. If your physical health does not allow you to sit still like that, you can prop yourself up in bed in a semi-

upright posture using pillows. As a last resort, you can lie flat with your back on your bed, but make sure you do not fall asleep. Once the posture has been taken care of, close your eyes.

2. Notice any noises outside of your room. Listen intently. Do not try to forcibly control the mind in any way. That would create tension when what you need is to relax. If you are practicing outside, notice the sounds of the surrounding areas.

3. Stay with the grosser sounds. If the mind loses interest in one of the sounds and it drifts off into thoughts, switch to another sound. It may be the sound of the wind outside, of passing cars, birds, etc.

4. Eventually, your mind will no longer have an interest in perceiving gross outside noises. At this time, try to hear subtle sounds within your room (in the case that you are practicing outdoors, try to listen to subtler sounds closer to you). These are sounds so subtle that usually escape your ordinary consciousness. If you cannot hear any, keep listening with intent. You may notice that you will begin to hear the sounds of your own body (e.g., breathing, heart beating, some form of tinnitus, etc.).

5. In due course, your mind will no longer have an interest in perceiving subtle noises either. When this occurs, the mind will inevitably want to escape towards thoughts,

dream imagery or sleep. At this time, remain conscious of the blackness in front of your eyes until the time is up.

b)

You should apply the same method, but instead of focusing on external sounds, you should place your focus on physical sensations until your mind exhausts the need of being aware of them.

1. Sit comfortably in a straight-backed chair, sofa, mat, or on a meditation cushion. Notice any physical discomfort, and adjust your posture accordingly. If your physical health does not allow you to sit still like that, you can prop yourself up in bed in a semi-upright posture using pillows. As a last resort, you can lie flat with your back on your bed, but make sure you do not fall asleep. Once the posture has been taken care of, close your eyes.

2. When you are truly comfortable, stay with the first physical sensation that you notice. Perhaps it is the pressure of your body where it makes contact with the ground, mat, chair, bed, or meditation cushion.

3. Stay with that sensation until your body gives off signals of pain or discomfort. When it does, adjust your posture to make it comfortable again.

4. Once that is done, stay with the first physical sensation that arises.

5. Notice that soon enough, pain/aches creep up once more. These are fundamentally caused by the mind and will keep surfacing over and over again as distractions. This time, do not adjust your posture, but instead, focus your attention on these sensations.

6. Stay with these sensations until your mind loses interest in them. When this occurs, switch to another physical sensation.

7. Eventually, your mind will no longer have an interest in perceiving physical sensations, and will inevitably want to escape towards thoughts, dream imagery, or sleep. At this time, remain conscious of your breathing until the time is up.

This preparation will help to desensitize both external sound and physical sensations to a certain extent. It is also a way of getting the mind and body accustomed to having some minutes of your day entirely dedicated to being with yourself.

Schedule:

Practice at least twice per day, 5 to 20 minutes for about two weeks. Be aware that you do not need to become extremely proficient in this practice. Use it as a means to reduce distractions in the principal practices that follow.

Phase One: Laboratorium

Laboratorium is a space dedicated exclusively to occult or mystical practice.

It can be a whole infrastructure, such as a Temple, an entire division within a house, or a small space within a division.

It is up to the student to choose according to his possibilities. Notwithstanding, even a small space within his room, perhaps separated by a curtain, a screen (room divider), or something of a similar nature, is enough.

The Laboratorium has the purpose of facilitating the transmutation of the student's mental state. If a student arrives home from his job or from daily life in general, his common mental state of being will probably be very shallow, wandering around mundane matters.

The environment of a Laboratorium conditions the student's mind to be meditative. Just like someone might feel sleepy if they go to bed even if they weren't sleepy, the student will feel motivation and inspiration and will be in the correct state of mind to practice just by entering into the Laboratorium. It is the ideal place to practice.

Procedure:

Here is what the student should have in his Laboratorium:

- A chair, a meditation cushion, or a mat if the student favors practicing lying down.

The student should practice while sitting in a comfortable position. It should not be too comfortable that he falls asleep, but it should not bring any degree of discomfort. Sitting on a chair or on a meditation cushion with the legs crossed are the best options. As a last resort, the student can practice while lying down on his back, preferably not on his bed to prevent the mind from falling into the usually conditioned reflex of falling asleep. Something like a yoga mat is preferred to laying down on the bed.

- Any object that helps the student calm down his mind without making him over-externalize his attention is good.

E.g., A candle. This is particularly beneficial if the student uses this item as an object of focus in the next phase. This object is also a universal symbol of meditation and calmness. Even if the candle is not the object used in the next phase, it's still an excellent choice for any Laboratorium. Turn off any lights and let the natural flame of the candle illuminate the area. This sets up the ideal environment for occult practice.

Another item the student can use to make the room more suitable to practice is burning incense. This also helps to soothe the ambient. However, make sure the fragrance is not too strong that it turns into a distraction.

Fundamentally, any item that helps to prepare the mind to enter into an environment conducive to practice is good. Anything that distracts the mind must be disposed.

The same is valid for sound. Some students favor practicing with some meditative music, nature sounds, binaural beats, or even with the sound of a water fountain.

Note: if you can't pick a noise-free environment due to outside noise, you can treat the outside noise as thoughts and therefore ignore them, use sounds as mentioned above, or you can use silicone earplugs.

All items used within the Laboratorium must be used exclusively in there. They cannot have any other purpose, otherwise they will lose their meaning and energy.

In addition, students with a more devotional disposition can also use an object that signifies their devotion towards God, or towards the Higher goal that they're trying to achieve. Before each practice, contemplate this object and its meaning for a few minutes to increase your devotion and therefore your motivation and inspiration to practice. This devotion-object must be treated just like all objects within the Laboratorium: with respect and reverence, making them sacred.

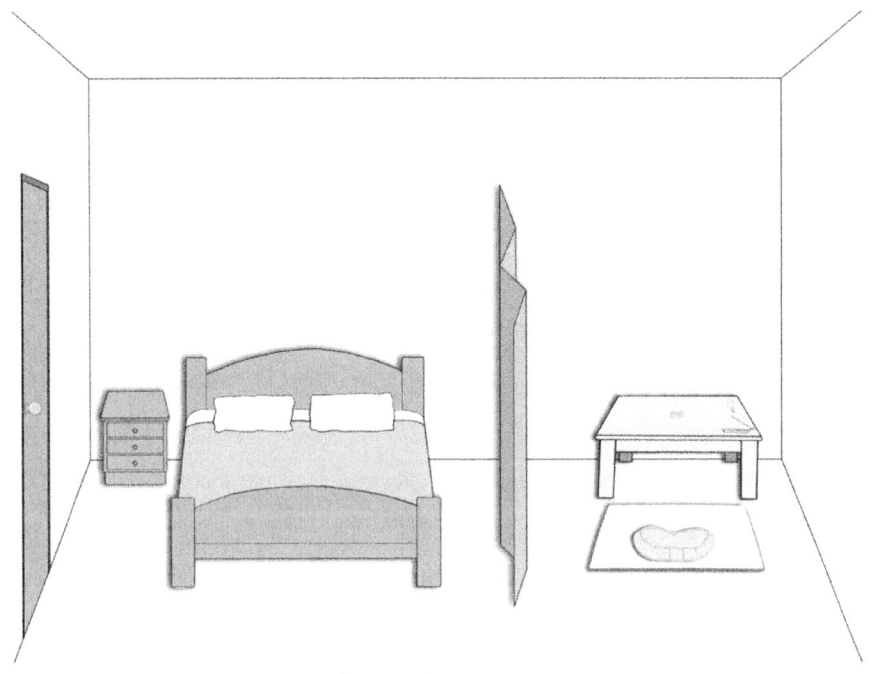

Example of a Laboratorium within a bedroom

Phase Two: Steady Inner & Outer Gaze

Like in all spiritual, mystical, and occult traditions, the student must have a firm grasp on the ability to sustain attention. In fact, in High Occultism, this ability is extremely crucial, being the core foundation of the whole practice.

This distinct type of attention can be named "Steady Gaze", and it is such an imperative facet of High Occultism that it must be sufficiently mastered before even attempting to go further. It is not only related to the external ability to focus the eyes but, more importantly, to focus the inner eye of the mind.

Attempting to practice the next phases without completing this phase first will significantly diminish the likelihood of success for the aspiring occultist.

Despite the value of logic, reason, and philosophy, the student must soon find their ultimate impotence. It is only by transcending the ordinary mind and its limited capabilities that the student can come into contact with the unspeakable stillness of emptiness. A flash of immortality can only be reflected in the empty lake of unmoving crystalline water.

Sustained attention and steady gaze (external and internal) must be gained in this phase. There is a relation between steady eye-gaze and the mind's ability to concentrate. Furthermore, steady gaze allows the dormant capabilities in the mind to automatically come into being.

To accomplish this, we will employ a straightforward tactic that any student can practice and reap great benefits. This is true as long as the student makes at least a modest effort.

Procedure:

1) First stage – Outer

The goal is to focus the mind on an external object. You can use any object you want (e.g., a candle, incense, a clock), including representational symbols such as *Aum* (ॐ), *Tetragrammaton*, *YHVH* (יהוה), *Yin and Yang* (☯), *Infinity* (∞), or any other sacred symbols. If you choose symbols rather than actual objects, they should be drawn on a paper and framed.

These symbols have an ingrained representational connotation and energy that act underneath waking consciousness. They are important because they correspond to and conjure mystical experiences that lie in potential within you and within the collective unconsciousness.

You must pick an object that is appropriate but without a strong emotional connection. Such emotional attachment could cause distracting thoughts and feelings.

You can pick a few objects to see which one is the most suitable for your practice, but once you've made your choice, remain with that chosen object. Continuously changing the object of focus will diminish the effectiveness of this practice. Choose carefully.

It takes a while for the mind to grasp the qualities and form of an object, and if you switch to a new object every week, that will not be enough time to enable the mind to adapt. Do not fall into the temptation of "this is not working; I will try another object". This is a recurrent motion of the mind to stop students from achieving more growth. Persistence is your ally in such a case.

A candle is a superb candidate because it is bright, mystical, and it can hold the mind's attention. On top of that, not only does it have an uncanny ability to steady both the physical eyes' gaze and the mental attention, but also leaves a vivid and clear after-effect image when the eyes are closed, which will be important later on. This is the best object for novices.

Possible Objects:

The best objects are bright objects. If the chosen object is not something immovable, it should be placed in line with your field of vision (at the same height as your eyes) so that you don't have to move your head up or down, which may produce pain or discomfort.

It should not be placed too far away either. Stretch your arm right in front of you. At the end of your hand, this is the correct length to place the object. This is the most natural position for the majority of students. If for some reason you feel that something doesn't quite add up, move the object to your preferred distance and height. In the end, it depends on the size of the object as well as the preference of the student.

If the student uses glasses, he should first try to place the object in a way that he can see it without needing them. However, if that's not possible, there's no problem in using glasses.

The reason to start with a physical object lies in the fact that the majority of aspirants are used to have their attention continually focused on external objects. Furthermore, the only time they close their eyes is when they go to sleep. As a result of this, they find it tremendously difficult to close their eyes and focus on an inner object. They usually become unstimulated and fall asleep.

This is the first barrier that the student of Occultism must overcome: the ability to focus the mind while having the physical eyes closed. We will employ the steady gazing on a physical object until the student's ability to sustain attention with the eyes opened improves.

If a student can't focus with his eyes opened, it will be impossible to do it with the eyes closed.

Yawning, boredom, dullness, the eyes closing and drifting off into sleep or dreaming may occur, but you must be persistent and keep them opened and focused on the chosen object.

Remember to relax the eyes to prevent them from flickering. Do not try not to blink. You may naturally blink to hydrate the eyes, but there may come a time that many minutes go by without blinking.

We actually want to achieve that because we want to train the eyes to enable them to gaze at the chosen object for a long time without unfocusing or distracting themselves by looking at other objects.

This will give rise to the after-effect image when the student closes his eyes.

Technique:

1. Place the object in the correct position and sit comfortably in a straight-backed chair, sofa, mat, or on a meditation cushion. If it's not an object that you are capable of positioning such as a tree, merely posture yourself correctly in a favorable position for steady gazing. The correct posture includes having the spine erect.

2. Relax the body.

3. Focus on the chosen object for 5 minutes with the eyes opened. Keep the mind focused on that point as if only that object existed in the whole universe.

You must be able to focus for 5 minutes straight on a physical object without disturbing thoughts before moving onto the next stage.

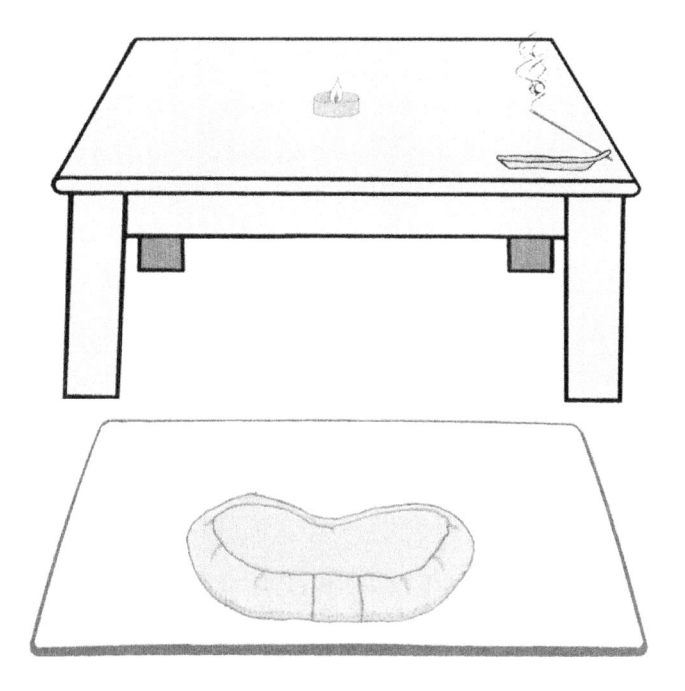

The Laboratorium of the student, using a candle as the object of practice

2) Second stage – Outer and Inner

This practice functions as the "in-between method", linking the Outer Stage 1 with the Inner Stage 3, which is solely of a mental nature.

First and foremost, the student should attempt this prefatory practice:

1. Relax the body.

2. Choose an object and place it on front of a white wall.

3. Focus on it for 30 seconds without blinking. The white

wall must be behind the object.

4. Now look at a white space in the wall where there's nothing but white. Notice how you see the object in negative colors.

When the student is successfully able to see the after-image in the white wall for ten seconds or more, he can advance to the actual exercise.

Technique:

1. Do the same beginning steps of the preceding stage.

2. Focus for 5 minutes on an object, preferably a bright object due to its ability to easily imprint its form in your mind when the eyes are closed.

3. Now close your eyes and see without too much strain, that the after-effect image of the object appears within the darkness of your closed eyes.

4. Gaze at the after-effect image of that object.

5. If correctly done, it will capture your consciousness within the darkness of closed eyes. This will, in turn, lead to a flowing concentration.

6. Stay with that after-image for as long as you can. In the beginning, it may escape your direct focus, so you need

to perceive it only through indirect focus or through peripheral awareness.

7. If you lose the image, you can restart the practice from point 2 onwards.

Given sufficient practice, the after-image will enable the conscious activation of the mind's eye. This means that what started as an after-image will now be seen with the mind's eye instead.

If the practitioner is already able to visualize the object with his inner eye, as if the object were really there, then he can do the same practice but without needing to do the stage of having to create an after-effect image.

If the practitioner doesn't see the after-effect image, there is no problem. It just means that more practice is necessary in the preceding stage.

If some vision or image arises, you can observe it but do not indulge in it. We want to train our equanimity of focus, and if you let the image engulf you, this purpose will not be accomplished. There will be a time for these experiences later on when the student is able to go through experiences while being emotionally detached.

If the after-effect image disappears, the student can open his eyes and look yet again at the object for some amount of time before attempting to see it with the eyes closed once again.

Do this practice for 10 to 20 minutes.

3) Third stage – Inner

The student should use the same objects or symbols, but this time, they are only to be seen internally.

1. Sit in your normal posture. There's no need for an external object this time.

2. Close your eyes and visualize the same object you've seen in the two previous stages. The aim is to focus the mind on an internal object (an internal visualization of an external object).

3. Try your best to visualize and keep that object in your conscious attention. There will be moments when you can easily see it, while at other times, only darkness will be seen. With that being said, because of the former training in the two preparatory stages, you should be able to sustain this visualized object for the chosen amount of time given sufficient practice.

This is the last stage and the most conducive to contemplation and occult meditation. This is because all ties with the external word are cut, unlike in the previous steps.

Do it until you can achieve 10 minutes of continuously seeing the object with the mind's eye.

Schedule:

Once or twice per day.

Do each stage until you graduate into the next one. Concerning the last stage (3), when you have attained the ability to hold a definite and steady image in your mind's eye for the designated amount of time, you can advance to the next phase.

Always practice in your Laboratorium and make sure you are not disturbed during the practice.

Possible obstacles:

Most students will have a confused and disorganized mind in the beginning. This makes it challenging for them to create and sustain an inner image that is powerful enough to seize the mind's scattering attention. The mind will always move the attention to day-to-day problems or "what will I do after I finish my practice?" type of thoughts.

Some students may believe that they have a great deal of difficulty in visualizing an inner object. They say they only see darkness. Let's explore why this is not really the case.

1. Close your eyes and try to remember what the door of your house looks like.

2. It wasn't that hard was it? You have probably seen the door without too much trouble. This means you can easily

see objects with your mind's eye. It's only required that you use your power of imagination. The difference is that it may be harder to do it consciously and when not using an emotional memory or an object that has a connection to you.

You will realize that the mind will quickly wander and forget the inner object. It's natural for a mind that is typically dispersed to divert its purpose onto other images or thoughts.

If this happens, return to your inner image as soon as you notice you are off track. If it happens repeatedly, it's best to return to the first or second stage and spend more time there. A physical object seen through the physical eyes is easier to maintain within conscious awareness due to its concrete nature. Concentration through the five physical senses allows the mind to hold its attention much clearer and steadier than through the mind's eye (inner object).

If you blink too much during the initial stage, the after-effect image will not be clear, and it will be hard to see it when the eyes are closed in stage 2.

Notwithstanding, you must not force your eyes not to blink. Even if you can focus for only 5 seconds, that time will inevitably increase as you practice more.

When you are focusing on the after-effect image with the eyes closed, if they move, the image will also seem to move. Consequently, always keep the eyeballs steady and unmoving.

Ancient memories may spring up during this technique, and you must understand that this is due to the process of purification. You are penetrating deep into the mind's unseen layers. Do your best not to move so that your attention does not get distracted.

The result:

Some eye-catching experience may happen to the diligent student.

Peace of mind and a deeper meditative state may arise from this practice.

This phase is enormously relevant and should not be neglected. It will open the doors to the latent contents of the mind that will be explored and put to use in the next phases.

The ability to concentrate will improve tenfold. The more the mind is scattered, the more we are restless, therefore, when the student is capable of keeping it steady at a single point, peace of mind ensues.

Our memory is also improved as a consequence, because our ability to think, recall and process are sharpened due to both the higher transparency in the mind and the power of concentration.

The eye's muscles will also be trained, and eyesight might improve, depending on the student.

This technique can also be used as a stepping stone into acquiring divine abilities, which rather than being pursued independently, occur as a consequence of rigorous practice.

Phase Three: Burning the Shadow of Fear

If the student of Occultism wants to delve deep into the mysteries of Creation, he needs to let go of everything that holds him back. Mainly, emotional responses based on fear.

Experiences within the realm of the occult can be quite intense. An unprepared student might become scared or be emotionally affected by them. For this reason, the student has to acquire a profound knowledge about his own psyche first. This requires introspection and contemplation.

As a preparatory practice, do the following:

- Write down your known fears;

- Keep in mind the intention to be conscious of what kind of fears you experience in daily life. Additionally, watch how you reacted in those situations. Then, write these fears down as well.

The mind must be exhaustively cleared of its negative associations and obstructions. The student has to go to the root of his being to discover what undermines the entire fabric of his self, in order to uncover the rapture which is the innate aroma of the Occult: the gem of God.

Procedure:

This phase will help the student clear off various parts of the subconscious mind, including childhood wounds and emotional disturbances.

This is critical because those subconscious traumas may become enormous barriers to the student, both in practice and life.

This stage climaxes in the in-depth exploration of the negative contents of the mind. Eliminating this negative energy will also significantly diminish the chance of the student encountering parasites in nonphysical realms that feed off our negative thoughts and emotions.

By delving into the subconscious, the student will directly face his weaknesses, foundational thoughts, suppressed issues, and emotionally charged experiences. The appalling facets of his mind should not be repressed once again, but instead, should be released by letting them arise, be, and disappear. This is a three-part process.

If a student attempts to suppress these underlying issues, they will merely subside into the subconscious and either arise at another time or invisibly mold and control our behaviors and attitudes in life.

On the other hand, if he acknowledges the existence of the trauma, and does not attempt to reject it, (allowing it to be), the trauma will lose its emotional strength over the student and eventually, given sufficient practice, subside.

This is an aspect of Occultism rarely mentioned in traditional texts, due to its apparent non-occult nature, being almost therapeutic. Do not let such words deceive you; this stage is a critical aspect of High Occultism practice. If a student does not undergo this phase, there's a chance he will have a traumatic experience in Occultism because of or related to fear. Fear brings tremendously negative energy that serves as a magnet for non-benevolent entities and such.

Technique:

Pick a known fear that you've previously written down. The known fears will be easier to clean than those that spontaneously emerge during practice.

1. Assume your meditative posture. If you practice lying down, make sure you do not fall asleep. Practice Phase Two (c) for about 5 minutes.

2. Relax. Feel your bodily sensations and notice if any body-part seems to be stressed. If you find a stressed body-part, focus your attention there and gently massage it with your awareness. Imagine as if you had astral hands and were massaging that area in a circular motion.

3. Keep doing it until all the body is stress-free.

4. Now let the energy of your fear emerge. Think about it or visualize it. Let it be in full scale.

5. Recognize that this is just a fear that has arisen in your mind, but it doesn't belong to you. It's a blockage that will prevent you from probing into High Occultism. Watch it with passivity, just feeling the raw emotions and sensations that it brings, trying your best to stay emotionally uninvolved. See it objectively rather than subjectively. Realize that the fear is not who you are. It's hovering around your consciousness, trying to affect you emotionally, but it is actually powerless.

6. That fear will eventually subside. Once it goes, notice how you feel and observe the bodily sensations for a few minutes.

As the weeks or months go by, and you keep on practicing, subconscious fears or old psychological damage will surface. Some of them you will have no idea where they came from (they may be from previous lives), while others you will have faint memories of them (childhood buried memories).

In this case, you must do just like in the central technique, but instead of focusing on the trauma that you want to clean, you will apply the procedure to this subconscious manifestation that has arisen.

You must observe the contents of your subconscious mind rise to the surface with emotional detachment, to the best of your ability. In the beginning, these experiences might be even stronger than the conscious fears and limitations that you have been cleaning beforehand (from the written list), but try your best to observe them passively, feeling the raw emotions and sensations instead of being absorbed into the traumatic feeling or memories that they evoke. If it helps, watch them as if they were separated from yourself.

By being conscious of the subconscious appearances with emotional detachment, you are utilizing a powerful weapon that will destroy the clasp that they have over your life. The very act of being conscious of them may be sufficient to brush them off the psyche.

At this point, due to the reasonably high degree of relaxation and concentration that you've achieved, you will be able to internalize your attention effectively. This internalized attention is pure and transparent by nature, which means it is lucid. Being relaxed and lucidly attentive, you can see the subconscious turbulence that arises with new wiser eyes, exhausting its influence over you. It's as if a higher intelligence within you takes over.

By doing this technique, the student doesn't remove the objective data, but rather the response to it: the subjective data. The subjective data is the emotional reaction to the objective data. Therefore, by altering the subjective data, the emotional turmoil associated with an ancient event in a person's life is deprived of emotional energy and consequently loses its power.

With no subjective data, that is, without an emotional

response to the data, the student destroys that limiting mental pattern. We are changing fear, anxiety, sadness, etc., with serenity. This purification is imperative in High Occultism.

This phase should not be restricted to the meditative practice only, but will naturally merge with life. Its positive consequences and closure may actually occur within events of daily life.

Take the following example:

There was a girl named Luna. She was an only child, and every summer she played hide and seek with her cousins when the family reunited. She was eleven years old at the time.

She really loved that game, and she was usually very good at it. One time when they were playing, and her cousin was counting, she decided to hide in the small pantry in the garage. In a rush to hide, she closed the door without remembering that it did not open from inside. She didn't even give it a second thought.

Once inside, and realizing what had happened, she decided to frantically knock with her little hands on the door calling for her cousins and parents. It took about ten minutes before they noticed her screams, but in her mind it felt like an eternity, imprinting a deep scar in her psyche. During that time, she was in shock, totally petrified, and hopeless.

Over the years, Luna always unconsciously sought open spaces. However, what she was most terrified about was about being closed doors in small areas, similar to being claustrophobic, although she was not well aware of this fact because it lied buried in her subconscious mind. She instinctively never put herself in a position that would make her feel confined again.

When Luna was 26 years old, she joined a mystical community and frequently did meditation/practice in the community's prayer temple. This was a small and dimly lit place that had only a candle to illuminate it.

One evening, she was so engrossed in her practice that time flew by in a flash. A member of the community, whose responsibility was closing all the common rooms after all members went to sleep, did not notice Luna inside the small temple, and closed and locked the doors.

As soon as the doors closed, their sound triggered the emergence of old subconscious remembrances. In her mind, all the memories and emotions associated with that childhood trauma surfaced. For one second, her heart stopped. Were she not an assiduous practitioner, she would have probably experienced a similar fear and uneasiness as she felt when she was younger, which would then be suppressed and hidden in the subconscious yet again.

However, because of her constant practice throughout the months and devotion to a higher purpose, her mind reverted to a position of calmness nearly in an instant. This allowed her to experience the same raw emotions, fear, sensations and memories from her childhood, but this time with a clear mind. They appeared, they were not rejected, and soon they dissipated. Luna had seen through them.

It's 5 A.M. The member responsible for the opening of the doors opens the prayer temple and finds young Luna in the center, meditating with a smile on her face.

This is a perfect example of how life and occult, mystical or spiritual practice merge to help uplift the student's state and eradicate his problems.

Schedule:

Once a day for no stipulated amount of time. Make sure you have nothing programmed afterwards because this practice can take anywhere from 5 minutes to hours.

Possible obstacles:

This phase requires great commitment and strength to confront and overcome the flood of subconscious problems. Some experiences may dishearten the student, but everyone should remember what's at stake: the Ultimate.

The result:

This technique leads to a calmer and more peaceful mind

by dissolving mental blockages, negative emotional connections and childhood issues. It also opens up the student to be more receptive to joy, natural mental abilities, occult and mystical knowledge, and overall, to a better quality of life. A higher and nobler ideal and a harmonious lifestyle are inevitable consequences of this practice. The world will be perceived with more clarity and transparency.

As it has been said throughout this chapter, the student will have a greater chance of not facing any issues when practicing Occultism or interacting with nonphysical beings if his psyche has been polished to a certain extent. This phase has numerous advantages, and it is one of the main differentiators between regular occultism and High Occultism. The benefits are endless.

Phase Four: Infusing Vital Energy

This phase is about focusing and charging each energy center with vital force.

To have power, fuel is required. This fuel is the energy that travels through each being's energy body. To use it for occult or mystical practice, the student needs to consciously control it.

The human energy body has an intricate design. It makes the connection between the physical body and the mind, and it comprises various energetic pathways that support the physical body with vital force.

These energy centers have to be developed due to the new higher demands that will be put on them through our Occult practice.

Accumulating Energy:

Human beings typically take in a minute amount of the energy that is available to them during the day. They do it mostly through food and the sun. At night, they sleep to restore the depleted energy.

Through a clear-cut occult, mystical or spiritual practice, the student can recharge and gather new energy. This newly acquired energy will be used for occult practice, increasing the power of his consciousness.

The student's energy body will then adapt and evolve to

attain a new level of functionality capable of sustaining new energetic demands moderately fast, given that the student puts the necessary effort into the correct practice.

Procedure:

This practice requires the knowledge of the location of the seven main energy centers (called *chakras* in eastern traditions):

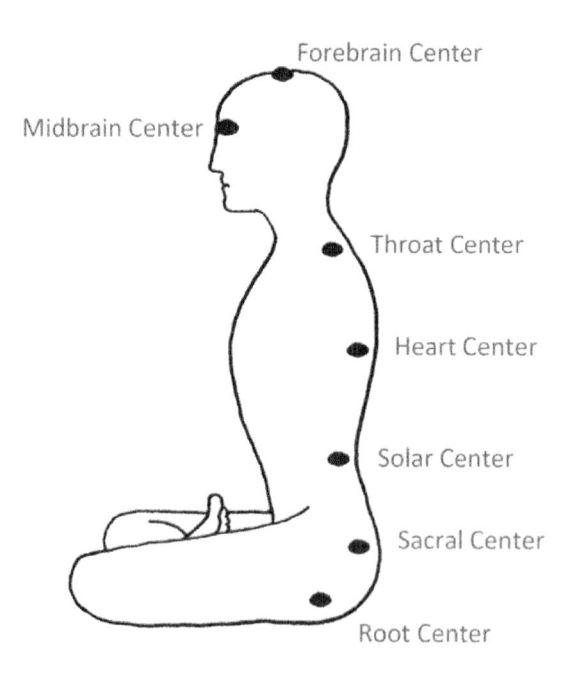

Technique #1:

1. Assume your standard meditation posture.

2. Close your eyes and place your attention in your Root Center. Let it dwell there for about two minutes.

3. Now move your attention to the Sacral Center and stay there for about two minutes.

4. Do the same for the remaining five energy centers. See the illustration to know their placement. It should be done through inner sensing.

This practice should take 14 minutes overall. In the initial stages, we are merely trying to get acquainted with the energy centers' presence, but as we go further, we want to charge them with the energy of our full attention.

Technique #2:

After being familiarized with the previous technique, the student can proceed to this one:

1. Place yourself in your standard meditative posture.

2. Close your eyes and feel the vital force within you. You may feel tingling all over the body, goosebumps, shivering energy through the spinal cord, or any other of the many possible effects.

3. Try to trace that energy to where it comes from. Find

its source, the universal vital energy. Notice that your vital energy is just a small part of the grand and vast universal energy, just like the space inside a jar is but a small part of the universal space that fills the whole universe.

4. Once you are able to feel the source of the vital energy, even if it's a faint feeling, try your best to absorb energy from there (this source is purposely abstract so that your mind does not conceptualize it). The absorption process depends on where we are storing that energy:

If in the Root Center, absorb red colored energy. See the red energy coming from its universal source to your Root Center and accumulating there. Keep doing this until you feel that your energy center is full.

5- Do the same for the other energy centers:

Sacral Center - Absorb orange colored energy.

Solar Center - Absorb yellow colored energy.

Heart Center - Absorb green colored energy.

Throat Center - Absorb blue colored energy.

Midbrain Center - Absorb indigo (halfway between blue and violet) colored energy.

Forebrain Center - Absorb violet colored energy.

You will be charging and accumulating energy on your

energy centers in each step. The color is used to make the visual process more alluring, and to help build a better connection with each energy center, considering that each one reverberates in a different frequency that is associated with a particular color from the Visible Light range of the electromagnetic spectrum.

This energy will make his consciousness more powerful allowing it to achieve deeper states and penetrate the occult mysteries.

Take this example:

If you eat when you are weak and hungry, you start rejuvenating and gaining new energy. This energy comes from the food that you ate which is being processed through the digestive process.

When you are weak and tired, if you go to sleep, once you wake up, you are rejuvenated and with new and fresh energy to tackle your day.

This occult practice will provide new and fresh energy similar to the two examples just mentioned, even if the student is initially unaware of it. This new extra energy will be used for spiritual and mystical progress in the student's journey to become a High Occultist. This is why it's fundamental.

The student may experience some ecstatic feelings during this technique because both the recharging and movement of the energy within the spinal cord and its energy centers are known to cause currents of pleasurable tingling, which can even elevate the student's being to a state of euphoria.

Possible Obstacles:

As the student begins his energetic work, some disturbance will inevitably occur. New energetic pathways in the nervous system will be created while old ones will be deleted. This process may cause some inconveniences, such as feeling depleted, tired, dizzy, or feeling pains, aches, etc. The student doesn't need to worry if any of these symptoms occur, because they are temporary and shall eventually fade.

They may occur owing to the fact that expanding and improving our vital pathways and energy centers requires a great deal of energy, alertness, and focus. The mind and body will naturally need to draw the necessary energy from somewhere.

Energy that would otherwise be applied in repairing the body, doing elaborated mental processes, digestion and so on, will be used for Occultism. This is why it is so critical to increase our ability to store and sustain a stronger energetic body. As the student's ability improves, the body and mind will be more alive, fresh, full of energy, etc. Drawing energy from the digestive process, muscle repairing, and so on will no longer be required. The abundance of energy will even improve these processes, and the student's body will feel better and there will be less need to sleep as a result of the higher energy levels that are available.

Schedule:

Once or twice per day. You can do Phase Two for 10 minutes before this practice if it helps you become more focused and calm.

Duration: 2-6 months.

Technique #1: 14 minutes, 2 weeks.

Technique #2: 30-60 minutes, 3-6 months.

If you feel depleted due to the high energetic demands of *Technique #2*, reduce the number of minutes that you stay in each energy center. It should be a gradual progress of conditioning the energy centers and enhancing the vital pathways. Progress slowly but surely.

The Result:

Once this process is undertaken, the vital force will flow faster, stronger and more freely, promoting a healthier and stronger physical, energetic and mental bodies. The immune system will also be strengthened as a side-effect of this whole procedure.

This phase is vital for deep inner-world practice and deep trance states (next phase), besides enhancing all benefits achieved in the previous steps. Lots of experiences may ensue from this practice, each according to each energy center.

There will be multiple rewards to the student who strives to practice this technique successfully:

- Improved physical and mental health;

- May sleep less hours;

- Higher vitality and energy levels;

- Magnified sense perceptions;

- Cultivating the arising of spontaneous mental abilities such as clairvoyance.

- Achieving a higher state of consciousness that allows more profound trance work.

- Etc.

These are side-effects of long-term energy work, and the timeframe and degree to which each student will achieve them will vary according to one's predisposition, persistence in practice, lifestyle, karma, etc.

Ultimately, this process requires time and commitment. Progress will mostly occur very slowly, but an aspiring occultist shall never give up.

Phase Five: Inner Laboratorium

Everyone has read or heard that the human mind is remarkably powerful. However, that power lies in potential until the student of Occultism is capable of harvesting it. The requirements are simple: having a calm, silent and focused mind, and being emotionally detached.

The ability to overcome the steady stream of thoughts and have a focused mind has been developed in Phase Two.

The tempestuous emotions, destructive subconscious thoughts and fear have been dealt with on Phase Three. The mind should be calm and focused by now. Notwithstanding, to go even further, the student has to meditate directly from and in a subtler dimension of the mind instead of doing it from the waking consciousness in the physical world.

To accomplish this, the practitioner needs to go through three stages:

1. Relaxing and using the power of concentration to enter into a deep trance state, disconnecting from the physical body.

2. Out of the body, the practitioner will use specific portals to achieve a connection to the universal collective unconsciousness and interact with archetypes and other types of beings.

3. These beings will then teach him specifically according to his path. Nevertheless, the practitioner must learn how to differentiate between his imagination and actuality. There's a thin line between these two when he's in these subtler dimensions because the latent powers of creation in the mind are active. We will give you clues to help to distinguish between both.

Procedure:

Any willing student is capable of effortlessly creating the most intricate scenarios in his mind. Even those that claim that they cannot successfully visualize anything will not deny that they can build elaborate fantasies or imaginations in their mind's eye.

Imagination is also connected to memory. If you have ever lost anything such as your house keys, you likely attempted to replay these actions in your mind to recall where the keys were lost. This is similar to using the creative powers of imagination. It's a natural and innate ability within the human mind. Everyone can do it.

Preparation:

Read the whole preparation before attempting it.

Put down this book or the device where you are reading it and go drink a glass of water. When you do it, be aware of all the steps you take, all the corresponding physical sensations and how you feel inside.

Now that you've had a glass of water, sit or lie somewhere, close your eyes and relax.

Try your best to recreate what you just did: stopping the reading, getting up to get a glass of water, drinking it and then coming back to where you initially were. Do this with your mind's eye. Feel all sensations (walking, the pressure of your feet on the floor, grabbing the glass, the taste and freshness of water, etc.) and replay the whole chain of events in your imagination. Feel as if you are really doing it in real time.

Realize that you don't actually "see" these images as you imagine, but you can somehow perceive them with your mind.

Afterwards, you can also (and should) attempt to imagine different scenarios to work out and connect with the subtle five senses, engaging the visual, auditory, tactile, olfactory and gustatory sensations.

Example:

See yourself walking barefoot on the beach on a beautiful sunny day. Notice how the sand feels in your feet, how the fresh breeze touches in your body, and the warm sunlight on your face.

You can create as many scenarios as you want to practice the power of your imagination.

Main Technique:

Read the whole technique before attempting it. All steps should be memorized in advance.

1. Take your usual meditative posture.

2. Close your eyes and take 10 deep breaths. Each time you exhale, feel yourself increasingly letting go and becoming lighter.

3. Now imagine vividly that there's an elevator in front of you. You enter into it and it starts going down. Mentally feel the falling sensation in your mind, as if you were really going down or falling.

Keep going down into your subconscious. You can look up and see a distant point becoming smaller and smaller, further and further away. This will eventually change the brainwave activity from Beta (awake) to Theta (asleep).

An example of the elevator's door.

Do this for around 20 minutes, or for how long it needs to take you into a state of profound relaxation. The time it takes to enter into a deep trance depends on your level of experience, ability to relax and let go, and on the power of concentration.

4. As soon as your body becomes very heavy, like a rock, you are in a trance. It should feel like everything got calmer, vaster and more tranquil. There may be a pleasurable humming quality in the body, and it will seem like you are far away in a distant world. The five senses have been withdrawn from the external world, and your attention is focused exclusively within. There may also be perceptions of coldness, slowness, and sensations of being afloat in a void or dark space. The ultimate sign of being in a deep trance is that you will not be able to move your physical body: it is totally paralyzed. You should aim to reach this deep trance state.

5. The elevator has now arrived at the bottom, and it is now located inside your Heart Center. See the doors of the elevator opening into an open area.

6. Now, imagine that there is a big temple in front of you. This temple has a stairway that consists of seven steps. On the top, there are two primary columns, one white, one gray, and six other columns, three on each side. The white column has the symbol of the sun, while the gray column has the symbol of the moon.

On the entrance, there are two big golden doors. There is also an eight-pointed star on each door, inside a rhombus.

The frontispiece has the symbol of infinity within a circle. See the illustration below to have a better idea.

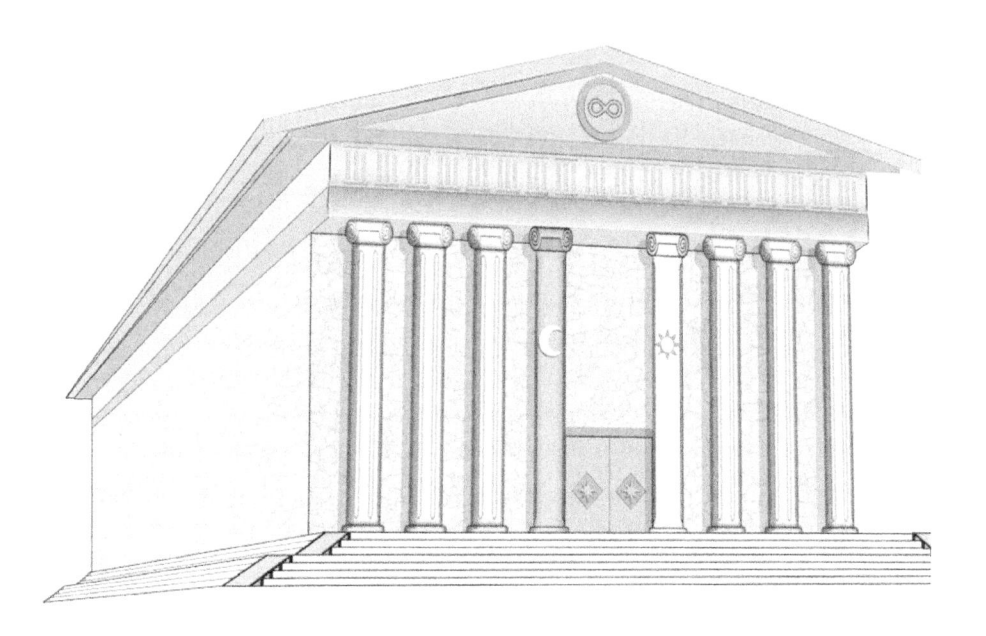

We will call this temple: The Inner Laboratorium.

Symbols and their meaning:

Eight-pointed stars: all paths go towards God. All directions go towards and come from the same center, which is the Primordial Substance.

Circle: Symbolizes God; no beginning and no end.

Rhombus: Symbolizes the higher Self. A prism converts all colors (the lower self in each different life) into one unified Light (the higher Self).

Infinity: Symbolizes the infinite nature of God.

2 Primary columns; Moon and Sun: the two polarized energies mentioned in chapter 11 that we have to unite.

Eight Columns: The eight elementary facets of Existence and Creation in High Occultism mentioned in chapter 7.

7 Steps = The seven primary energy centers.

There is also a deeper meaning in these symbols which we will let the student find out by himself.

7. To enter into the temple, put each of your hands on the eight-pointed star on each door, and pronounce *Fiat Lux!* (Let there be light). Both doors will then open.

8. Inside, there is a tremendously strong white luminosity in the air. There is a bright Golden Sphere of Light in the center as well. This sphere symbolizes your inner Master.

9. Thank "Him" for being there by contemplating and absorbing golden energy from Him for some minutes.

10. When finished, bow in gratitude and leave the inner Laboratorium. Open the door from inside and close the door from outside. Then go downstairs and walk into the

open space. See the elevator appearing and opening its doors. Enter it and feel the sensation of elevation or of going upwards. Do the reverse of what you did in step three.

11. Gradually start coming out of trance until you reach waking consciousness. Open your eyes and proceed slowly and with care after this practice, because some parts of your body might either be dormant or unresponsive for a while.

Repeat this practice every day. The more you do it, the easier it will be to be absorbed into the whole scenario and vividly experience it.

Schedule:

During the first month, ignore anything that happens out of what has been stipulated in the instructions. Even if you see entities inside or outside the inner Laboratorium, or if the Golden Sphere of Light does anything, ignore everything. Your inner Master (represented by the Golden Sphere of Light) will understand.

This is important because it will condition your mind to the whole process, consequently erasing any possibilities of it making things up. Although this method begins by using imagination, you will soon recognize that anything that happens within the temple is actually real and not imagined. We are employing imagination as a portal to a subtler inner dimension.

After one month, continue to ignore everything that happens outside the inner Laboratorium, but do not overlook anything that occurs inside it anymore. Take anything that happens inside it very seriously. This temple is your inmost home.

Make sure you write down what happens inside the inner Laboratorium in a personal journal so that you can consult it later on. Some events will not make sense initially, but after some days, months or even years, they can become clear and be understood. Therefore, having a journal to write them is essential.

Possible Obstacles:

Fear is an enormous barrier, but you have learned how to deal with it and in Phase Three.

You may experience sleep paralysis during this practice (the body can't move yet you're wide awake), but you just have to move your toes and you will come out of it.

It might be hard to experience or perceive the subtle dimension of the Heart Center with clarity, but this ability to use and emerge into the subtle senses will improve with time and practice.

Don't try to see with your physical eyes. If you do, you will only see blackness. You have to see as you saw on the Preparation stage. It's perceiving without seeing. Given sufficient practice, you will begin to truly see with the subtle eyes of your mind, and the same goes for all the other senses.

Thinking that what you saw within is a fantasy of your mind will not take you far. It is not a fantasy. It's worth repeating that you use imagination as a portal, but after crossing it, it takes a life of its own. Once you truly experience the inner dimension of life, all doubts shall disappear.

Having expectations or wanting something to happen is an obstacle. That's why the previous phases are given special importance. You need a calm and focused mind instead of one that wants to see something in particular or control the practice to achieve a specific outcome.

As soon as you enter into the inner Laboratorium, everything that you experience must be natural. Do not attempt to control or create anything; let everything appear effortlessly.

Do not attempt to recreate something that happened in a previous practice either; do not reject messages or insights that you receive during this practice, nor try to dismiss your intuition. Reflect on these insights instead. Try to decipher their meaning. You can apply them as your object of concentration as you've learned in Phase Two (c).

The Result:

Due to this practice and to the interactions in the inner world, you will receive profound messages and instructions. Be enthusiastic with your practice and keep developing a relationship with your inner Master. With time, He can acquire a form for a myriad of reasons, such as to communicate a message in a better way for you.

What happens within your consciousness is now an adventure for you to explore. Use your nonphysical body or your "point of consciousness" (if you don't seem to have an astral body) to explore and engage in whatever occurs there.

Mental powers, visions, predicting the future, etc., can happen during this practice. Notwithstanding, they are not the signal that the student has completed this phase. This practice should be employed until there is no more an inner Master because He and the student have merged into One. That is the hallmark of success on this stage, and it can take some years. More about that on the next phase.

This practice can originate sensations of dizziness, light-headedness, or a slight pressure in the stomach and Solar Center areas (a stronger version of the so-called "fluttery" sensation). These energetic sensations are due to the impact that the trance state and this practice have on the energy body of the student. While in a trance, this method can also cause spontaneous out-of-body or astral projections. If that were to happen, the student could either return to his body or if he's feeling good, he can do a minimal exploration of the surrounding areas. Ultimately, this practice induces a bilocation of consciousness from the physical body to the subtle body within the inner realms of the brain and Heart Centers.

Divine Infusion

When you are comfortable entering into your inner Laboratorium, you can do a practice that is similar to Phase Four, but a more effective version.

All steps stay the same, except for the first few steps:

1. Place yourself in your standard meditative posture.

2. Close your eyes and do this phase (Phase Five) and enter into your inner Laboratorium. Once you are inside, place your astral body right in front of the Golden Sphere of Light in the same meditative posture as you physically are.

3. Ask the Golden Sphere of Light, which symbolizes your inner Master, to bless you with divine energy.

4. Focus on the Root Center.

Absorb red colored energy directly from the Golden Sphere of Light into your Root Center. Keep doing this for a while until you feel that it has abundant energy. You may feel tingling sensations in your Root Center, among other sensations. This is normal, and it will happen to all energy centers.

5. Now do the same for the rest of the energy centers until each one feels like it's full. This is excellent to recharge and store divine energy that can be used for a multitude of purposes, the highest of them being the unveiling of the Occult.

6. In the end, show your gratitude by bowing towards your inner Master, and then leave the temple.

This is a more powerful version because you are absorbing energy directly from your inner Master, which symbolizes God, rather than a more abstract (and difficult to connect with) Universal Source that may be difficult to "perceive".

Optional – Inner Requests

After practicing this phase for at least three months, you can begin to ask questions to your inner Master.

You can inquire him about your life but beware if your mind is not calm and empty of mind chatter, his response (which may come in many ways) will not be entirely grasped.

Furthermore, you may not get an answer. It depends on countless factors, so it is best you do not expect it, which is always beneficial because it also makes the mind more open to any spontaneous answer.

You have to trust in your own ability to be receptive to the answers, and must not let doubt arise. Doubt can destroy all possible ways of understanding the answer, just like a parasite will in due course destroy its host.

Here are some types of translations that the mind can use for answers: spontaneous thoughts, images, soundless sounds and real-life events in which you know are a direct response to your query.

You should try to refrain from asking mundane questions, and should instead pursue only your higher ideal, the ultimate goal of unveiling the Occult.

Additionally, requests may also be asked, but their delivery will always be dependent upon the student's particular journey into Occultism and degree of mental freedom to allow the necessary receptiveness.

Phase Six: Inner Union

By this phase, if the student has done everything according to this book, his external Laboratorium will be full of tangible energy and presence. Sometimes, some auras, halo effects, magical sights or apparitions may occur. This is because this particular place has been charged with a high amount of energy, thereby possibly transforming astral energy into physicality.

In some extraordinary cases, some nonphysical beings may even temporarily manifest, as if the subtle astral dimension had been superimposed on the physical realm. The student should not be in a state of expectancy concerning these types of rare materializations but should open to such possibilities.

Union with the Inner Master

Before enrolling on this stage, the student must reflect attentively and confirm that he has fulfilled the previous phases' objectives. If that is not the case, the student must go back and try his best to achieve what is lacking from earlier phases. All of them must be concluded in their entirety before attempting this last phase. Take the necessary amount of time and effort to undeviatingly but regularly work through all sequential phases. They are simple but can take many months to accomplish each.

There are different levels of union with the inner Master.

In the beginning, each student will see "Him" as a Golden Sphere of Light, but after some months of diligent practice, He may take a form according to each student's predisposition and devotional-religious background.

If a student has always seen Jesus Christ as a divine figure of wisdom, the inner Master may take Jesus Christ's form. The same may happen to those fond of Gautama Buddha's teachings, or of Mohammed, Krishna, Shiva, Moses, Angels, Archangels, Devas, Gods, Deities, and so on. This form is a representation of God. The form taken by the inner Master will always be the one that fits the student's character the best.

After much contemplation and practice in the inner Laboratorium in His presence, the student will finally merge with the form of his inner Master.

If this union takes place, the student will progressively start to embody his inner Master's qualities, virtues, gifts, characteristics, and perhaps even some divine abilities, among other possibilities. The student's life will be wholly changed by transforming his own consciousness into the highest representation of divinity in this world.

If there is no particular fondness for any specific form in the student's latent subconscious, the Inner Master will remain "abstract" as a Golden Sphere of Light.

In this case, the student's union with his inner Master will be slightly different. Rather than slowly embodying a particular mannerism, virtues, qualities, etc., the student will progressively embody universal characteristics of divinity, such as inner peace, joy, unparalleled wisdom, powerful intuition, and perhaps some divine abilities as well, which are always dependent upon the student's destiny and life's purpose. All of these are contingent on the personal inclinations of the student, and also on the collective human consciousness.

Both types of union symbolize a higher state of consciousness. It is being one with what is usually called "Higher Self" or "OverSoul".

No particular practice has to be prescribed to achieve this union. The student has to practice the previous phases with determination and focus, and in the end, deeply contemplate his own higher consciousness that is symbolized by the inner Master.

Beyond the Form of Divinity

The next step is one of the most laborious in the path of High Occultism. It must be understood that a representation of divinity, regardless of its degree of purity and manifestation, is always limited by its own assumed form.

This implies that the student has to overcome his own Higher Self. This a very secret teaching, and exceedingly challenging to communicate.

The student has to invert his own form into no-form. This is the real vacuum of emptiness, of pure potentiality. The student has transformed his limited being into a higher form of being, a pure expression of divinity. He went from personal lower self to the universal Higher Self. Notwithstanding, this Higher Self has to be transcended as well, into the pure no-self dimension.

The Higher Self, being the purest manifestation of the Primordial Substance, must turn back on itself into pure potentiality, before there were even a lower or higher self. This is the realm of the highest form of Occultism.

Now the occultist must not imagine, see or attempt anything, but just sink into the void of emptiness. Promptly, he will feel an endless and direction-less void of emptiness. It is here that the Ultimate must be found to unravel the highest mystery of Occult.

The occultist must not despair in this life-long journey, because one critical realization he will certainly have: God is unknown by any human means, and He will always be so. Our inherent union with Him is our knowing of being the Unknowable itself: the unlit Light.

14

Interaction with Nonphysical Beings

To the common man, the whole subject of the existence of nonphysical beings, let alone the interaction with them, will appear to be an absurdity and a byproduct of a fertile imagination. However, to the student of Occultism, they are known to be real. Sometimes, such beings might also be symbolic representations of different archetypes, entities, higher intelligences, and even other unknown types of supraphysical beings.

Most of them are autonomous and hidden forms which lie beyond ordinary human consciousness but can be "accessed" through the conscious mind of one who achieves a high degree of occult ability, such as entering into a deep trance state and fulfilling all of the previous phases' requisites.

This is certainly not a fairy tale as the student shall find for himself. Innumerable mystical and occult books throughout the ages have talked about it: evocations, mediumship, materializations, seeing spirits, astrally projecting out of the body to other subtle dimensions of consciousness with the purpose of interacting with different types of lifeforms, etc.

A person whose mind lacks the necessary training to use the power of subtle perception will never accomplish the magical conquest of consciously communicating with such beings.

Most people are only concerned with a life of materialism, so these higher subjects and conquests are completely outside their spectrum of understanding and experience.

There are occasional cases when people have unexpected mystical experiences with nonphysical beings. This can be credited to their journey and accomplishments from previous lives.

Interaction with nonphysical beings must not be jumbled with mediumship. Although both could be termed "occult practices", and both develop trance states, there is an immense difference between them.

Interacting with nonphysical beings occurs in a higher state of consciousness. When the student's waking consciousness infuses the subconscious mind, this interaction becomes possible. This state is a level higher than waking consciousness; it is active and positive.

On the other hand, trance mediumship is a state below waking consciousness. During such states, the subconscious mind of the medium serves as a vehicle for the nonphysical being. This being then invades and manifests through the medium's waking consciousness, overlapping it with its own consciousness. This is a passive and negative state.

Procedure:

At first, the student may not perceive the nonphysical being with much clarity, but upon continuous repetition of this practice, his mind will develop the necessary abilities to perceive anything with the most intricate detail and clarity.

If the student attempts to perceive it with his physical eyes due to habit, he will not be able to see anything. This is a natural tendency that needs to be overcome through ceaseless practice.

The method lies in doing your usual procedure to enter into the inner Laboratorium and from there attempting to connect with the being that you've chosen, inviting him to come there, so that the two of you can interact.

For best results, it is best you utilize the feeling of presence of that nonphysical being. By feeling it, you are asking the being to come to your home. This is easy to do, as long as you know its energy or feeling of presence.

By this stage, even if it is an unknown being, you will be able to feel that being's energy and presence merely by reading its name, thinking its name, meditating on its symbol, seeing its visual representation, etc.

This is the easiest way to call a being into your inner Laboratorium. Take notice that you should only attempt it after you've reached and are comfortable with Phase Five, else there's a high chance you will be met with failure.

Everything that you see here does not imply that these things are objectively like that. What it means is that your mind is translating the energy from those encounters and explorations into something perceptible that can be understood, in parallel to the symbolism attributed by mankind's collective consciousness.

For example, if you see a library in the astral realm with countless books, that does not mean there's really a library in the astral realm. It's merely how your mind is translating that energy. What this means is that your mind perceives that there's a lot of knowledge and wisdom in that energy, thus presenting you with the objective symbolism of a library.

Likewise, an encounter with a nonphysical being does not imply that the entity you are connecting with has that particular form or mannerism. It is your predisposition and the message or teaching that the being wants to convey that makes it assume any particular form or setting, therefore facilitating your understanding.

Some occultists or mystics prefer that students do not openly initiate communication with unknown beings, for the most varied reasons. This is a safety measure that we certainly support.

Notwithstanding, the difference in communicating with them through this method lies in the fact that within the astral walls of your inner Laboratorium, nothing bad can happen to you. In fact, that's your safest place in the whole astral realm, because the inner Laboratorium's frequency is extremely pure due to being "located" within the nonphysical Heart Center. This is not related to emotions, feelings or any of the so-called "emotional attributes" of the heart, but rather, it is related to pure love, peace, sincerity, harmony, and sacredness. This is the home of the Higher Self, The Guardian Angel, the Inner Master, the Oversoul, etc.

With this in mind, you can attempt to communicate with spirits, entities, and so on, given that you address them with respect and sacredness. If that is done, there's a chance they might come.

Low-frequency parasites or mischievous entities will not be able to enter in your inner Laboratorium but will attempt to persuade you to leave its walls to meet them. Outside of your temple, you are on your own. Understand that the higher your spiritual frequency, the higher the types of beings that may interact with you.

Some low-astral entities can't even get close to your inner Laboratorium, just as a fly can't get close to a flame: if it does, it will burn to death. In some occasions, however, such beings may attempt to convince you that you cannot enter into the inner Laboratorium in that particular day, or that they are blocking the entrance. This is utterly foolish, and you should never believe in them. They are merely trying to feed you negativity so that they can trick you and suck off your energy. Once you manage to enter the very first time into your inner Temple, the doors are always open and unblockable, even if they appear to be closed, or if some entity appears to be in front of the doors, "blocking them".

An easy way to distinguish between such beings, for those who aren't sure, is to feel that particular being's presence. There are numberless higher intelligences, some with good intentions, some with not so good, but the purity of heart never lies. If that being lacks a presence of love or peace, then that's not someone the genuine occultist has interest in interacting with.

Through this practice, the student may meet marvelous beings that will share the most striking lessons, teachings and experiences. Many secret and magical practices may also be taught to the student, some of which may help him in his path towards God, some may be just ways of fully using mental abilities and the latent powers of the mind.

The first-hand experience of this type of encounters is priceless. The occultist will be able to store many of these experiences in his conscious mind and use that knowledge to benefit humanity in the physical dimension. Sometimes these encounters and experiences will, unfortunately, remain in the subconscious mind, and the occultist will not be able to remember them except when certain events happen in day-to-day life that trigger the surface of those hidden memories. Maybe such an encounter has already happened to you, and you don't remember it, although there's always a slight feeling of something that you can't explain lingering in your mind.

Once such a fully-conscious experience occurs, deep impressions and unbreakable insights will forever sculpt the occultist's soul. It's truly life-changing.

Evocations

There are also the so-called "evocations" of spirits. Be that as it may, High Occultism is not concerned with those manifestations. A High Occultist interacts with such beings directly in his own inner Laboratorium, or in their subtle territories, instead of trying to physically evoke them or trying to have some physical manifestation of their presence. High Occultism is hence a higher form of contact with non-physical entities.

Through this method, however, there is a way for the student to achieve a similar purpose as in those in evocations.

Given sufficient practice, the student's mind will be able to overlap the interaction with the nonphysical entity into physicality, therefore enabling the student to appear to actually physically perceive the immaterial being.

Notwithstanding, the truth of the matter is that nonphysical beings are never truly materialized, therefore their connotation of "nonphysical" beings (if they were to materialize, they would no longer be a nonphysical being).

What occurs is that the student is able to be both in the physical and in the astral realm at the same time, superimposing one on the other, and by mixing both realities, it will seem as if, for example, a spirit is being physically perceived.

This is common with hallucinations, or with "seeing things that are not really there." Of course, here the occultist goes much further because not only is the visual and auditory subtle senses superimposed on the physical counterparts, but even the touch feeling can be activated. It is a difficult achievement, but not outside the realm of possibility.

It can be said that this attainment is a natural consequence of practice, and enables the student, within limits, to interact with nonphysical beings without having to be in a deep trance state. It is not something actively pursued but may happen to the diligent student nonetheless.

Final Remark Regarding Calling Beings Outside of the Inner Laboratorium

Be cautious, blindly calling for unknown beings may not be the best action. If you want to call unknown beings, always do it from the inside of your inner Laboratorium. That way, any wicked entity will be blocked from interacting with you.

On the other hand, if you are outside of the inner Laboratorium, for example, in an out of body experience, and try to encounter a nonphysical being, the type of encounter comes down to your energy. If a student has negative or selfish intentions, his low mental frequency will match entities of a similar low frequency. That's the kind of entities he'd be inviting into his presence. If a student has genuine or loving intentions, that's the kind of beings he will attract too.

If you are unaware of what kind of beings you should contact, ask your inner Master. He will provide you with an answer, though perhaps not in the way you would expect.

If you are curious, you can also proclaim within the walls of your inner Temple, "Spirits who have something to communicate to me, if your heart is pure, you may enter!" or "May those whose heart is pure and full of divine wisdom bless me with their presence and teachings!"

Ultimately, you must be aware that anything any being can teach or share with you, your inner Master can too. It's up to your Inner Master to let messages, communications, experiences or teachings be brought by beings other than Himself, for whatever reason He sees fit.

SECTION 4

Going Forward

15

It is Not a Coincidence

The student of Occultism knows that there are no coincidences. Coincidence or chance are just expressions designating an inability to recognize a cause. This inability may be due to the ignorance of the student or to the occult nature of the cause itself.

Because of this, most people cannot realize that there is a continuum between all events. There is always a pronounced chain of causes behind all events, even if it's just an apple falling from a tree. There are no coincidences.

Considering this, the reader must be aware that it is no coincidence that he is reading this book and these words right now. All the efforts that you've made in your current life as well as in past lives have brought you to this very moment. This is not an accident; a higher intelligence has brought you here; God has brought you here.

If you were able to look back, you would notice that an infinite chain of seemingly arbitrary events has culminated in this very moment.

Every thought, action, feeling, and word has its immediate and posterior, direct and indirect consequences. Through occult practice, you are aligning your inner values and mindset with a higher state of consciousness which allows you to discover the only thing that breaks free from this infinite chain: God.

God is causeless, the cause of all things, and all things themselves. This is the only way a student can break free from this cosmic domino.

Enrolling on the study of the Occult is the highest decision an aspirant can make, and one that can change his life forever.

Most humans unconsciously meander through their lives, being imprisoned by their culture, jobs, environment, and their very own lifestyle. They are influenced by their family, friends, and apparent figures of authority, as well as by the way they think of themselves and of what they believe others think of themselves. Their desires, emotions, perspectives, moods, and expectations create limiting barriers that inhibit them from becoming true occultists.

The fervorous student will not fall for such things. By knowing how Creation works, the path towards the Creator, what to expect and how to overcome any obstacles that may arise, such a student will reach inward into the universal mind, uncovering the most incredible mysteries ever imagined by humanity.

Such an accomplished occultist is not subject to a higher power anymore like a typical human being, because he has risen above the superficial dimension of life, leaving blindness behind forever. He consciously is the High Power itself.

16

The High Occultist

Beset with sorrow, Man tries to find his way out of misery. However, commonly, humans born and die without tasting the natural divine rapture of life.

The advanced student, on the other hand, is a powerful center of consciousness, like a star shining with its own self-made light. There will be no chaos, incongruity, distress, problem, anxiety, uncertainty, worry, boredom, greed, and lust in him once he truly transmutes himself into a High Occultist, because then, he'll be grounded in the core of a higher state of consciousness, on the abode of true knowledge.

The occultist has not forsaken life and the world, hiding in his magical cellar, temple or Laboratorium. The real High

Occultist has unleashed the principle behind Occultism: the imperceptible yet existent unified field that sustains everything: God.

Through occult and mystical practice, the student will open the gates to his celestial essence, finding his home in the unseen, yet more real than the seen.

The energy that allows the occultist to express himself comes from this very hidden field, deep within his consciousness. Creativity, power, knowledge, wisdom, intelligence, joy, peace, tranquility, empathy, compassion, kindness, sagacity, generosity, etc., compose both the inner state and the demeanor of an occultist of the highest caliber. We have left behind witchcraft, superficial occultism, ritualistic-based lifestyles and dogma, and have risen above the surface. The student now breathes fresh air, filling his lungs with the utmost exquisite and indescribable realization.

Humanity as a whole must head in this direction. It is by the training and discovery of what Occultism is that those adepts who have discovered it will give birth to a new era on planet Earth.

This is the highest enterprise that any student should aspire towards. Besides the discovery of countless beings in infinite nonphysical dimensions, besides the interaction with mysterious forces and miraculous events, besides the awakening of supramental capabilities, and the new sagacious outlook towards nature, life, death, spirit, and God, it is on Earth that we currently are. By this directive, we can go to the highest of heavens, but we must certainly descend into our human form once again at the end of the day so that we can fulfill our purpose in this world and accomplish what we are supposed to accomplish.

The High Occultist truly has the keys to the mystery of mysteries: he has unraveled the Occult's essential nature.

Epilogue

Meditate on the fact that you've come a long way through the reading of this work. More importantly, put into practice the lessons hereby taught. Despite performing them and acquiring much wisdom, power, out-of-this-world raptures, traveling nonphysically to subtler dimensions of consciousness, meeting other types of beings, interacting and perhaps even becoming one with his Higher Self, the Occultist must be aware that there's still a great deal for him to apprehend, realize and actualize.

Bowing in awe to the complex yet magical Creation that befalls upon every one of us, together with having overcome both superficial desires as well as the mystical pride of being "an initiate", the humble High Occultist must pierce into God's infinite realm of being, embracing the unknowable mystery of eternity.

Want to read more books like this? Show your feedback with a sincere review, or send an email to the author at mysticsarom@gmail.com, telling him what you thought about the book and what you'd like to see in new books (more mystic, occult and spiritual content, sharing more knowledge regarding practices, divine abilities, metaphysical explorations, etc.).

Subscribe to Gabriyell Sarom's Newsletter and receive the book:

Divine Abilities:
3 Techniques to Awaken Divine Abilities

www.sacredmystery.org

Publications

The Art of Mysticism

The Step-by-step practical guide to Mysticism & Spiritual Meditations

The Art of Magick

The Mystery of Deep Magick & Divine Rituals

Suggested Reading

- **Christian Mysticism**

A Course in Miracles by Helen Schucman

A full mystical guide from novice to advanced. We suggest it for those who are acquainted with the Christian terminology.

- **Eastern Mysticism**

Kundalini Exposed by SantataGamana

We normally never endorse modern books, but this one has genuine depth and wisdom concerning Union with God and the vital force.

- **Western Mysticism**

Initiation into Hermetics by Franz Bardon

A classic text to become familiar with western magic and mysticism. It contains a practical guide.

- **Mysticism & Philosophy**

The Hermetic Philosophy of Ancient Egypt and Greece by Three Initiates

The essence of the teachings of Hermes Trismegistus.

Printed by Amazon Italia Logistica S.r.l.
Torrazza Piemonte (TO), Italy